M000197579

Why Do I Scream at God for the Rape of Babies?

The story of Princess Moonbeam is a difficult story to read,
but it is also a story of courage and hope.
Our story will take only a few hours for you to read,
but it will hopefully change your life. [1]

Why Do I Scream at God for the Rape of Babies?

~

Claudia J. Ford

Thank you for supporting South Africa's children. love, Claudia

NORTH ATLANTIC BOOKS
BERKELEY, CALIFORNIA

© 2004 Claudia J. Ford. All rights reserved.
No portion of this book, except for brief review, may be reproduced, stored in a retrieval system, or transmitted in any form or by any means—electronic, mechanical, photocopying, recording, or otherwise—without the written permission of the publisher. For information contact North Atlantic Books.

Published by
North Atlantic Books
P.O. Box 12327
Berkeley, California 94712
www.northatlanticbooks.com

Cover design by Paula Morrison with Susan Quasha; text design by Susan Quasha
Printed in The United States of America
Distributed to the book trade by
Publishers Group West

Why Do I Scream at God for the Rape of Babies? is sponsored by the Society for the Study of Native Arts and Sciences, a nonprofit educational corporation whose goals are to develop an educational and crosscultural perspective linking various scientific, social, and artistic fields; to nurture a holistic view of arts, sciences, humanities, and healing; and to publish and distribute literature on the relationship of mind, body, and nature.

Library of Congress Cataloging-in-Publication Data

Ford, Claudia J., 1954–
    Why do I scream at God for the rape of babies? / by Claudia J. Ford.
       p. cm.
    Includes bibliographical references.
    ISBN 1-55643-547-9 (pbk.)
    1. Ford, Vyanna, 2001– 2. Ford, Claudia J., 1954– 3. Child sexual abuse—South Africa—Johannesburg—Case studies. 4. Infant girls—Violence against—South Africa—Johannesburg—Case studies. 5. Gang rape—South Africa—Johannesburg—Case studies. 6. Adoptive parents—South Africa—Johannesburg—Biography. 7. Mother and infant—South Africa—Johannesburg—Case studies. 8. Sexually abused children—Rehabilitation—South Africa—Johannesburg—Case studies. I. Title: Why do I scream at God for the rape of babies?. II. Title.

    HV6570.4.S6F67 2004
    362.883'092—dc22

2004018092

1 2 3 4 5 6 7 DATA 08 07 06 05 04

*This book, and therefore, my life,
is dedicated to my loving mothers:
Tina, Elsie, Vivian, and Sondra;
and my gentle sons:
Juma, Tiba, and Tai.*

ACKNOWLEDGMENTS

I HUMBLY THANK PROFESSOR PAM NICHOLS, the Director of the Writing Centre at Wits University, for an unprecedented degree of professional and personal support to make this book a reality. Pam, you must know that your critical eye and loyal encouragement of my writing efforts made this possible. I would also like to thank my colleagues and friends, Greta Berlin, Charlene Smith, and Margaret de Pavarachini, for their support for both the book and my family, which is always instrumental and deeply appreciated. To my sister-friend, Toyomi Igus, I continue to be awed by the love and connection, and three decades worth of friendship. Toy, you have always inspired me as a writer; you are a mentor and a role model. To Richard and the team at North Atlantic Books, thanks for your patience and support. To my brother Clyde W. Ford, thanks once again for lighting the way and for your timely advice as a more experienced writer. To my goddaughter, Ayiko Carmichael, a reminder that it's always a pleasure to have your completely subjective opinion of my writing skills—your love and devotion sustains me. To Susanna Napierala and my midwife sisters—you have always taught me, by example, the meaning of true inner strength. To my daughter, Sandra Mncube, more than anyone, I could not have done this without you. To the Goddess Club—what would I be without your love? My heartfelt thanks.

Foreword

On December 2, 2001, a late spring day in the southern hemisphere, my daughter, who had just turned five months old, was cut open with a broken bottle and brutally gang raped, then left to bleed on a dirty mattress in a rundown porn theatre in central Johannesburg. It doesn't matter that on December 2 I had not yet met her, that I would take this little infant into my arms by the side of her hospital crib on December 10, and bring her to my home on December 13. On that sad day in the Action Cinema she was still my daughter. She was my daughter, she was your daughter, she was our daughter....

Our inability to protect her from this heinous crime was our collective failure as adults to protect our children. How did we let this happen? I grew up in America in the 1960s, in a generation that was characterized by our unrelenting, potent criticism of adults. Whom, now, do I look at to criticize? Where can I point an accusatory finger? It's me. It's us.

I imagined when I arrived in Johannesburg in 1994 that I had adopted the newly born country of South Africa to make a difference in its democratic transformation, to use my professional skills to make an impact on nation building. In that desire was an enormous challenge. Indeed, in relocating to South Africa I took on a temptation to my skills as a healer, equally suspecting that I would use my professional and academic acumen. How, then, was I to know that a little eight-kilogram moon-faced bundle of bottomless eyes, miniature colostomy bags, and liquid antiretroviral medications would show me that perhaps the most important skills I had to offer my new country were my patience, my nurturing, my ability to recall or make up the words to nursery rhymes?

This small journal of remembrances is a love paean to my daughter, named Nolothando by her birth mother, re-named Vyanna, and affectionately called Princess Moonbeam by me, her adoptive mother. I wrote these diary entries and interwove them with my poems, letters, and academic papers during the first two years of our relationship. It was an exceptional, emotional two years of doctors and hospitals, tears and frustration, unremitting exhaustion and the ceaseless joy that comes from surrendering to the love and care of a small child.

Only three short days elapsed between meeting baby Vyanna and taking her into my home. It was quickly apparent to me, however, that the rhythms and cycles of my unusual, peripatetic life had already prepared me for such a momentous change. I realized with bottomless gratitude that I brought to this task of healing a damaged infant the good fortune of a strong education, the parenting legacy left to me by my mother (who died in 1989, with her doctorate in early childhood education), the experience of raising three sons, already grown, as well as a home and financial and emotional security.

I swiftly realized that my professional training as a midwife was invaluable for the medical skills I needed to take care of this infant thrust suddenly into my arms. Somehow, even my development career, which had taken me and my sons to every corner of the globe, had prepared me to accept and understand change, to witness inexplicable atrocities, to see beauty on the hidden side of irreparable damage, to live in awe and gratitude for the chrysalis of life's lessons.

Yet, with all my resources brought to bear on juggling the healing of a broken child, my work at the university, and the multitudinous bureaucracies of post-apartheid South Africa, it was not enough. One year of hauling myself through the offices and hallways of social services, children's courts, public hospitals, and the departments dealing with fostering and adoptions left me reeling with the acute awareness of my own privilege combined with a growing need to make sense out of what had happened to my daughter.

If I struggled with this Fabian safari then how must other parents feel, much less resourced than I? What could I say to my daughter when she grew old enough to ask? That I walked away from the issue of child rape in order to concentrate on taking care of her, fully knowing that other little girls were going through this same descent through hell?

I discovered that I had to speak out. I reached deep into my own troubled past to find the courage to fly in the face of the contrary opinions and concerns of my closest friends, and the general public silence, and to stand up against the abuse of children. But this journal is not about my courage, it is about the extraordinary circumstances leading to the intersection of two lives—mine and my daughter's. Hence, it is about my past, a present that we are creating together, and her future. It is about my heartfelt desire as Vyanna's mother to give her a future that allows her to fully reclaim her childhood innocence, so brutally and incomprehensibly ripped from her that dark day in December 2001.

Why do I speak out about this vile and violent deed? Because I want to be able to look my daughter in the eyes and tell her that what happened to her will never happen to another little girl ever again, and that I was outraged, and that I loved her enough to do something about it, to honor her unheeded screams and her raw courage by speaking into the silence....

July 1, 2001

I CRAVE THE BLANK PAGE. Lines, no lines. Possibilities, no possibilities. Emptiness. Boundlessness. Limits. For once. For a rare, perhaps a first time, I am faced by my own limits. I am face to face with emptiness that spills like faceted jewels into a deep pool of absolute stillness. My geometrically skewed words are swallowed up by the stillness, not a ripple remains. I have nothing to say. I have too much to say.

I don't know what to say.

Once upon a time. That's easy. That's the way all stories start. At least all of my childhood stories started that way. Once upon a time.

Once upon a terrible time. Once upon a dark time in the worst slums of Johannesburg, New South Africa, Rainbow Nation, Mandela Land. Is that how your story starts?

Once upon a time, there was a Princess. She was born in the ordinary way to a young woman who was very, very poor. This young mother was so poor that she had no shoes, no place to live, and no food to eat. She only had a very tiny, very special, very beautiful little baby girl, gently smelling of almost-ripe peaches, the color of fresh caramel, with tiny rosebud lips. This young mother was so poor that she never noticed she had just given birth to a Real Princess.

December 1994

REBEL DAWTA

within each fragment
embedded in each chapter, is the whole of my life
the whole truth
the whole of pain and loss and survival
the whole of hope, love, and triumph
to understand a piece I must reveal
the complete patchwork tapestry that is my life
I must tell my story

every scrap of silk, cotton, sack cloth, and newspaper
no, even the threads—visible and invisible
that hold these scraps together
must be told
the fabric's beauty cannot be otherwise explained
every rent, stained, and soiled fragment must be
unfolded
every masterful patch of craft and art must be
displayed

with the warp and weft of my pilgrimages
I have chosen from the opportunities offered
wisely and foolishly I have torn the fragile threads
while committing to my own life
I have burned ephemeral bridges of cloth
with the simple acts of choice and praxis

those closest to me say
I am running away from life, from myself
they are wrong of course
I am running, yes
towards life, towards home
to embrace myself
and I find myself everywhere
and I dance in the arms of all I have met and worked
with
can I be blamed for that

to understand fully you must know that the adventure
always begins with a journey

December 10, 2001

A child forsaken, waking suddenly,
Whose gaze afeard on all things doth rove,
And seeth only that it cannot see
The meeting eyes of love.

MIDDLEMARCH

ENTERING YOUR HOSPITAL ROOM, I feel as if I am on tiptoes. Hushed. Reverent, as if before the soaring of the thirty-foot stained glass windows in a New York City cathedral. Awe. Inspiration. Silence. As well, I am filled with an inexplicable dread. Do I know what evil looks like? Do I dare know what the residue of dark foul deeds will look like clinging to an innocent infant child?

I try to pacify my errant feelings by becoming intellectual, clinical, medical. I hide my fear behind my bedside manner. In hushed and dreadful silence I stride on tiptoes into your tiny hospital room. Scared and curious I feel my heart beating in my throat, too quickly. I try to breathe in slowly with a state of awareness and mindfulness. I transform. I am The Midwife. Observing. Assertive.

Your bedside is cluttered with official-looking people doing things to you and for you, women and men wearing the uniforms and impedimenta of their jobs. Stethoscopes, notebooks, cameras, needles, and charts. Nurses, journalists, doctors, social workers, and police. I ache to push the others roughly out of my way and beat a path to your crib. I turn around instead to wash my hands in the cracked enamel basin in the corner of your room, losing myself in the calming, familiar ritual of soap and fingers.

December 12, 2001

FOR THE MILLIONTH TIME IN THE LAST TEN DAYS I have felt like crying—this time at last, it is salty tears of joy that sting my eyes. Today, during my usual frantic early morning session with the laptop, email, dishes, laundry, and other multitasking housework, I told the boys—your foster brothers, Juma, Tiba, and Tai—that you would be coming home, and that they would be pressed into physical and psychic duty as The Ford Family Personal Baby Body Guard Service with special reference to Moonbeam Princess Nolothando.

Tiba, twenty-three, the middle child, wrote back immediately to let me know how excited he is about you joining our family. I am warmly pleased at this confirmation of the love circle I have created among my offspring—a circle you will now join—and this proof that I have raised three Gentle Men. It brings additional tears to my already brimming eyes. I will save Tiba's email for you to read when you are old enough. You must know that your unconditional love and acceptance into our small family was instant, immediate.

It is a soft, grey, and rainy day of the highveld summer variety. The air smells of wet earth, the dark tang of humus from simultaneously budding and decaying plants. It is a fitting day to bring you home, I suppose, as your light will only shine brighter against these skies that are like the feathery, fuzzy underbelly of a new kitten.

Already the controversy rages like Johannesburg's late afternoon thunderstorms—plotting in ominous circles of threat and release. How much should I tell you? From everything to nothing at all. The debate has begun to spin like dust devils. Who else should know? From everyone to no one.

I have decided to explore the depths of my own heart in this matter through my writing. I stretch the canvas of this unforeseen, improbable, unknowable circumstance through the familiar challenge of language. Painting my doubts, my outrage and frustration, telling what cannot possibly be formed with the inadequacy of lips, tongue, a palate too soft for such harshness. A syllabic brushstroke saying what cannot be heard with tender ears unused to such shrill, stiff, unfathomable notes.

December 13, 2001

WHEN I MET YOU ON MONDAY you were alert and watchful.
Cautious. Yesterday I drove to the hospital to see you again.
You were playful as a kitten. Courageous.

Eleven days ago, you were brutally defiled. Yesterday, when
the pediatric nurses were showing me how to change the
tiny colostomy bag, I took my first peek at your little vaginal
flower. It is already beginning to heal, and like you, it will
open shyly but determinedly to one day be in the full bloom
of confident womanhood that you deserve. I feel honored
to be asked to care for and heal the petals of such fragile
vulnerability.

Today, unable to sleep for my excitement at your
homecoming I woke at three a.m. Three in the morning,
that special time I normally reserve for packing up my
transoceanic trips, spreading the detritus of a professional
expatriate woman and her three children across my bedroom.
Packing, organizing, planning, containing the boundaries of
a life that is meant to be experienced within the space of six
suitcases. Three a.m., a time of focus and determination. A
time for the sleepy rooting of insistent newborn babies, for

unwanted important phone calls, for coffee and stacks of exam papers that must be marked.

Today I woke at three a.m. and began assembling your nursery in a safe corner of this multicultural colorful explosion of moments from my global travels that will soon be your home.

You are safe here, my baby. By being here you increase the protection that naturally surrounds this magic castle. The angels and fairies have delighted in your arrival. Just yesterday I glanced quickly up to see them scattering like twinkling fairy butterflies through the white curtains in the dining room. They are waiting, to dance around your crib and bestow their blessings on you, The Moonbeam Princess. The fairies' evil sister has already done her worst, and her presence and influence have been banished from your life forever. You are here to gracefully and regally collect your magic gifts. I pray I am worthy and strong enough to help you learn the humility of Praise Singing, and Joy, and to teach you the part about Happily Ever After.

December 14, 2001

You ARE A SMALL BUNDLE, lying peacefully on my bed, smelling of sun warmth and the innocence of spring daffodils, dressed in a pink pajama sleeper that is too big for your tiny body. The feet slouch off, the sleeves threaten to cover your precious little thumb. You protest. You drift in and out of sleep, and wake to babble to your patiently waiting teddy and dolly, then allow the heaviness of your eyes to take over. You are my child. How you bring back memories of my own childhood, still so fresh in my mind though many say that is impossible. I know you are aware and remembering everything. I will keep quiet about what I already know of your wariness with others, but I will talk to you.

Freeing you from the institutional clutches of the hospital yesterday afternoon was a major drama, a saga worthy of a Princess. My sense of anticipation and excitement was overwhelming by midday. My heart was racing without my bidding; my nerves were taut as cello strings. Every sensation was heightened. The afternoon sunlight was too bright. My axons confused taste with smell and touch with hearing, until I was breathing in the pulsing of the slanting light and drinking down air that smelled buttery like lemon pound cake.

Everyone who was meant to assist in the exodus was assembled in my house by three p.m. We had secured the permission of the director of the hospital for you to be released to my care as a "place of safety" and we were waiting impatiently for approval from the Chief of the Child Protection Unit. The social worker was ponderously slow, peering over the top of her wire-framed glasses at numerous different forms, dotting every administrative *I*, and crossing every bureaucratic *T*. Her compassion and matter-of-factness calmed the butterflies of my waiting-room expectancy.

I continued to experience an overwhelming desire to push away these people and their red tape and simply scoop you up in my arms. In the end, it felt like that was exactly what I did. I felt as raw, as empowered, as impassioned as a new mother, after my three-day pregnancy. The thought of you lying in that metal crib alone, unloved, was almost too much to bear. "Not a moment longer of this cold neglect," I kept saying to you in my head.

My journalist friends accompanied me to the public hospital, where we negotiated the impersonal maze of medical wards to find pediatrics on the seventh floor. I bundled you up in a green and white blanket with all your medicines, supplies, and toys, swooped out of the hospital with my feet barely touching the cold linoleum, and huddled with you in the back seat of the car for the fifteen-minute drive to my house.

I wanted to whisper to an indifferent world, "Look at this beautiful girl child, this miracle. Born of her suffering and her pains." It makes no sense that I felt so attached to you. I know that you are not mine and that I am only taking care of you temporarily for the State. Somehow, that doesn't matter. What I know in my head is disconnected, unplugged from the wild fluttering of my heart. I cannot imagine feeling more bonded to you. It is truly as if I have given birth.

December 15, 2001

WHAT A GOOD GIRL YOU ARE. You are too good, cautious,
tentative, not like a five-month-old baby at all. But your
courage is rising and you are cooing to me, and demanding,
and singing. You sleep at night from eight thirty p.m. to four
thirty a.m., my idea of a perfect baby. You eat voraciously,
and I am enjoying fattening you up with mashed fresh foods
and formula and love. You suck down your bottle with fierce
determination, even though I can tell from your sucking that
you were a breastfed baby. Not knowing your HIV status,
I don't dare try to breastfeed you myself, though my long-
unused nipples are now tender and swollen with their own
hormonal wisdom.

And too, you gulp down the nursery rhymes and children's
songs I struggle to remember, your black velvet eyes greedily
hanging on my lips, my voice; your tiny mouth attempting to
imitate mine, the sounds of this morning's doves flying from
your throat.

You were not too impressed with your first bath, pushing
at me with your tiny fists, a worried frown on your little face.
But then my Mommy skills are rusty—we will figure it out

with time and practice. The hospital staff was so kind to you and did the best they could.

Everyone's compassion and grief overflows in a torrent of pity and concern and searching looks at you, at me, as they take you into their arms and ask me in a hoarse whisper if I will please relate to them the details of your story. Once again. Your story is not your story, it is your old story, it is everyone's story.

God "slaughters the innocents" so that we will take notice.

I used to scream at God for allowing babies to be raped, until I realized that in allowing babies to be raped God was screaming at me.

I am listening, my little Vyanna.

December 1998

HEINOUS CRIMES

Part I

my young friends
a group of homeless ten-year-old boys
they sleep like puppies
curled around each other's rags on the cracked and dirty
   sidewalk
in the colonial part of old town
watched over by the faded and crumbling pink stone
   buildings
that have given it up
to the heat, humidity, abandonment, and neglect

I buy them apples, bread, and oranges
stroke their satin brown cheeks
and let them call me "mai"
at night I feed them imported cookies
and chocolates
to sweeten the cardboard box dreams
of my children

Part II

we keep our bathtubs filled with water
and lay in damp cartons of canned peaches,
beans, and bags of bug-infested rice
if the troubles of war reach us here in the city
how long before electricity and water
are restored
we stock up on batteries and torches
and wear our cell phones and two shortwave radios
in leather pouches and belts slung around our necks,
waists, and hips
we wonder if we will be able to tell the difference
between the roar of mortar, rockets, shells,
and the rumble of the thunderstorm
that comes daily with the bloody crimson sunset

Part III

they always take photographs or draw
their victims, man, woman, child, and infant
from Auschwitz, Toul Sleng, Kigali, Palestine, and
     Pristina
we know with certain chill the blank look
in human eyes of death coming

they leave a pictorial legacy of scorched, frozen, and
gassed flesh
torn nails, bayoneted, piked, and cutlassed babies

the bloody tortures they would carry out on their own
     families
throwing their lives into rivers and ditches and over
picturesque cliffs and hills

they force us to pull hard against the
slippery slope of human evil, heinous
crimes against our own humanity
once the beast tastes its own blood, released,
it is uncontrollable

December 17, 2001

IT IS YOUR TRUST THAT YOU HAVE GIVEN ME. Unearned,
unexpected, you have placed your quiet trust at the altar of
my lap, my mother's arms, and midwife's hands. You bring me
your five months of hell, your 195 days of hanging on a hook
in the Action Cinema. You grip the wooden cross of your
chaos and poverty in a chubby fist and lay it down at my feet
on top of used plastic shopping bags full of discarded plastic
colostomy bags, full of smelly undigested baby shit. Your shit,
your trauma, your despair, your innocence, your hope, your
trust: you pile it all at my feet and drift carelessly, heedlessly,
recklessly off to sleep in the middle of my bed.

When you finally fall asleep I am choked up with tears as I
keep vigil. It is when you are at complete relaxation that I am
assaulted by the true extent of your five-month-old innocence
and then the crashing reality of the incomprehensible violation
of that innocence. I am in an empty place, beyond words,
for those who hold you, and choke up, and look at me with
pleading eyes, begging, demanding, "How, Claudia? Why?"

I have no answers for them.

I whisper to you while you sleep the only prayer I know—
you are loved, you are safe, you are protected.

December 18, 2001

THEY SAY, "AT LEAST, THANK GOD, SHE WON'T REMEMBER," and I smile with patient compassion. I cannot rest in this assurance, no matter how sincerely given. You had been severely neglected for five months. You lived in a dirty, sad, and ugly place, full of drugs and alcohol, prostitution and the raw unpleasant odors of selfishness and despair, porn films and bare light bulbs burning at all hours, and uncomforting, grating, frightening noises. The day you were violated the feature film at the theatre was *Raped by an Angel*. This cannot be! Tell me which Angel! I will cast Him out of Heaven myself!

When you came home it did not take me long to realize that you had probably never been bathed. Your skin was rough, scaly, and dry, not at all like the soft downy velvet of baby skin. We knew you had not been fed properly and that your mother had left you completely alone in your theatre cubicle, for five, eight, twelve hours at a time. You taught yourself. You sucked your tiny thumb, you clutched whatever cloth was close at hand, and you never really slept. You watched, you were aware, even when I walked into your bedroom those first few weeks, your eyes would fly open immediately. You were hyper-vigilant. You had to know what was going on around you. You were determined to survive.

It took a few weeks of food, songs, and stories before you felt secure enough to really sleep. Then you fell into the ocean of deep and dreamless rest that belongs to babies, sinking into my down duvet and my love—your life raft.

Meanwhile I spent the hours in between mothering duties on the Internet. The research on infant memory is full of controversy. A pediatric neurosurgeon in Texas was particularly helpful. I read his work, and looked up his references. I understand that we tend to think of memory only in the cognitive sense, and therefore have no way to explain pre-verbal memories. I know that I have strong recollections of sense and people and place that were subsequently verified by my mother. I clearly remember the new tastes, the fascinating textures, the securely rhythmic noises, the shifting light and dark, the blanketed warmth and heaviness of infancy. I watch your face, your eyes, and I realize that you were, you are, observing and recording everything.

You may not remember, but I must assume that you might.

December 20, 2001

I AM UTTERLY AND COMPLETELY EXHAUSTED. My body, my brain, my soul are numb, heavy with a mindless tiredness. I have newfound empathy for new mothers, and realize that I am experiencing this profound stress without the screaming hormones and rapid postpartum physical changes that usually accompany such intense caregiving. How do we women do this? How on earth did I ever do this? Alone. Three times.

You remain a quiet, introspective, curious little girl. And oh, how you love your bottle, second only to that tiny thumb that you glue resolutely into your mouth for self-comforting.

I have come to understand the language of your communication. It is like the heady but faint smell of jasmine on an evening breeze—familiar, soft. I am still and go quiet to catch its deeper notes in my lungs with each breath. I have noticed that the more accurate my response to your emotional language, the more expressive you become. You let me know now when you are hungry, tired, bored, but also when you want company or to play.

Mostly you let me know when you need time alone. I must respect the fact that you are an unusually self-aware little girl—you spent so much time alone the first five months of your life. You have already learned to enjoy your own company. Your tiny fingers exploring the edge of your blanket amuse you for hours at a time. I consider this a good habit— you will undoubtedly look inward for answers to difficult questions. You will certainly get along with this reclusive, introspective family you have chosen.

December 23, 2001

Do children choose their parents? I always used to say so, half jokingly. Now, I look at you and laugh at my careless pronouncements. Have you chosen me?

By now the days are blending together in a thick caretaking fog. I have found your tickle spots under your unbearably soft baby arms and knees, and kissed you into hysterics on your chocolate belly and the velvety pleated folds of your neck. You like to take your naps on my bed, falling asleep while listening to classical music on the radio. I notice your sleeping getting deeper and more secure. You hate being woken at night for your antiretroviral medicines—you thrash your baby hands, tightly close your little mouth, and purposefully shake your head from side to side. I detest having to battle with you, especially as the medicine is now causing a horrible rash on your face. Fortunately just a few more days of the twenty-eight days of post-exposure medications remain.

I have learned to change your colostomy bag, finally, with the minimal amount of fuss. I don't mind the routine—as when performing any medical procedure, I am patient, careful, and organized. But I chuckle at the complicated instructions from my trips back and forth to see the stoma nurse. She must have completely forgotten that six-month-old babies don't lie still and cooperate. It's all I can do to keep your little hands occupied. I pin you spread-eagled under my legs, my hands free, singing endless rounds of "The Wheels on the Bus" to distract you. I suppose we do the best we can with One Mommy doing a Three-Nurse job.

Do they realize the unspeakable consequences of their actions? The men who have hurt you? The disfiguring rash, the uncomfortable colostomy bag on your tender skin, the difficulty getting you to bathe with the raw open sores, the every-six-hour medications to prevent you from getting HIV, the coming surgeries on your torn-apart vaginal floor?

Someone asked me what I would do if you were HIV-positive. That would be an unforgivable tragedy. But how could it possibly make a difference to how I feel about you? No, we would simply find a way to carry on.

December 26, 2001

You performed your role as the Christmas Child at yesterday's party as if you had rehearsed for a Nativity Play. You were quietly radiant in your little blue and purple party dress. A full set of double rainbows came out just before dinner, to complete the magic.

Now we are snuggled up in my bed together so that you can nap peacefully and get rid of the cough you have picked up from being held by so many strangers, and the damp air of Christmas night. Before sleep takes us on her gentle wings we sing and we dance and you already have a set of toys that you love to talk to. You can roll over and want to sit up and have finally learned to tolerate a few inches of water in the blue plastic dish tub that is your bath.

One more day of medication. I know I will feel less tired and numb when I can have a few uninterrupted nights of sleep. But you are a good baby and no trouble at all.

January 3, 2002

YESTERDAY I MET YOUR BIOMOM—your birth mother. I am
not sure how to begin describing her to you, except that
now when I look at your cute little face I see clearly that you
look so much like her. Only that her face is too old for her
twenty-four years. She looked tired, defensive, and hardened
by unknown hungers and her addiction to alcohol and the
craving for fast, late-night living that goes with poverty,
despair, and substance abuse. Her milk chocolate skin had the
oily, dusky hue of exhaustion and a diet of fizzy drinks and
greasy foods and neglect.

I was told by the social worker that if your mother did not
show up to the first court hearing we could press criminal
charges of abandonment against her. I had butterflies in my
stomach that nothing could get rid of on my way to Children's
Court when I realized that she might be there. I wanted her to
be there, I didn't want her to be there.

The Children's Court was in surprisingly good shape. I
expected it to be dirty and dingy, I don't know why. Instead it
was bright, the carpets were stained but an attempt had been
made to clean them, the walls were painted in garish colors
with Disney and nursery characters. The judges were behind

schedule and I sat for hours in the children's waiting room, on a faded low couch of indeterminate color, surrounded by huge stuffed animals and discarded dirty toys, watching a three-hanky Ricki Lake show about Adult Reunions with their Favorite Teachers and an entire episode of Telly Tubbies.

When I was finally called into the magistrate's chambers, I felt nothing but compassion for your mother. The magistrate was appropriately harsh. She had been scolding Nomsa[2] in private before I entered. After reading the formalities of the court order that leaves you in my care until "investigations" are over, the magistrate took an opportunity to commend me for taking in an abused and neglected infant. And then she turned to the other bench to further scold your mother.

Tired or hung over, and dressed in the clothes she had slept in, your mom looked more dazed than chastened. I suspect she understood much of the English being spoken, though there was also a translator for her. I can only imagine how I looked to her—a fat, well-fed, rich, colored-almost-white American woman. If only she knew or could believe that I, too, had had the experience of living on the streets with babies.

Actually, that is a harrowing story that few know and fewer would believe, but it probably would not have helped. I was desperately sad and often confused, but I was never ignorant or uneducated. I could always do better than torn pants and a dirty, stained T-shirt. I might not have adequately protected my own emotional or physical fragility, but I would have killed to protect the vulnerability and innocence of my children.

What kind of mother would allow her five-month-old daughter to be brutally raped by two of her drinking buddies?

I felt a small band of angels leave my heart in a light stream of cotton candy pink, as Nomsa passed me down the hallway after court. Even they may not be able to help her.

Nomsa did ask the translator if she would be able to see you. I'm glad she wants to see you.

January 4, 2002

FIFTEEN YEARS AGO, I gave birth to my third and youngest son in a tiny white wooden colonial house by the sea in tropical, humid Belize. It was an easy birth, beginning with tight pains in the morning, after eight. As soon as I realized what was imminent, unstoppable, I took a bath, lay down on my bed, became single-mindedly preoccupied with the rhythmic contractions of my uterus and by noon a little boy came gently into the world, surrounded by his amniotic sac, and dutifully watched over by his two brothers, nine and eleven years old. The Old Ones say that being born into his sac makes him able to see in both worlds at the same time for the rest of his life. It is true that your brother Tai has incredible sympathy, empathetic and psychic gifts.

When Tai was eight years old, we were having one of our continuing series of "sex" talks that characterized my sons' upbringing by a midwife. They had all seen condoms by the age of six, and had at least some vague notion of what they were used for. I knew enough as an experienced parent to wait for those unpredictable, transient but frequent teaching opportunities before broaching the "S Subject" as Tai, pretending to be very embarrassed, calls it. So it must have been something eight-year-old Tai said that prompted me to ask him, "Do you know what rape is?" He sighed (here goes Mom again), and answered without hesitation. "Yes, Mom. It's that thing that Mike Tyson did to that lady."

I smile about the childhood incident now, but the answer was accurate, and gave me the opportunity to press home one of my favorite messages about sex and respect. Afterwards I always wondered if I was the only parent in the world who said explicitly to my sons that "No" means "No!" I questioned if any fathers anywhere had ever said these words to their boys, or if my single-mindedness was related to my status as a single mother, and my own history of abuse at the hands of unkind men.

Now I suspect these discussions were not exercises in experimental parenting. Your presence in our lives sharply reminds me that I was purposefully trying to raise good men, and that I defined a Good Man by his ability to love, cherish, respect, and protect women and children. I always wanted to raise men that any mother would feel safe leaving her most precious daughter with. I succeeded. Three times over. Now I have my own precious Princess and I am almost frantic with the dawning appreciation that the task of raising good men was worthwhile beyond my wildest imaginings.

January 5, 2002

THEY GAVE ME THE WRONG BABY IN THE HOSPITAL! Those
nurses! They gave me a dirty, unloved, torn, broken, damaged
infant, smelling of unprocessed shit oozing from her waist,
covered with scaly rashes, globs of gelatinous medicine-
smelling mucus in her diapers. A suspicious, overly alert baby
girl knowing only the screaming of hard, wet, sharp, and
forcing objects and nothing soft, sweet-smelling, or pink.

You were traumatized and screeching in pain and frustration,
and I realized there was nothing I could do to comfort you.
I picked you up gently and held you so that you knew I was
there. Secure, but not too tight. I walked slowly with you still
screaming murderously, and whispered my mantra into your
tiny ear, "It's okay. You are safe. I'm here. I'm not going to let
anything hurt you."

I walked out into my courtyard garden and sat on the
cement bench by the koi pond's waterfall. When you got
bigger I put you in your pram and rolled you out to the
waterfall. We sat in the company of our silence. The sound
and movement of the falling water caught your attention and
forced you to come back to a place away from the dark and
bottomless abyss of your unnamed pain, your trauma and

despair. You stopped screaming. You got quiet. You watched and listened. You eventually calmed down and stuck your thumb in your mouth.

January 10, 2002

AN ADVENTURE. Yesterday we spent four hours at Johannesburg General Hospital in the public Children's Clinic. An experience I hoped not to have to repeat soon, but somehow I wanted to know what public health care was like, and I don't regret sitting there and observing. It was an all Black South African waiting room, about fifty mothers and fathers and siblings with children of all ages, mostly toddlers and babies, sitting patiently on long rows of wooden benches.

Two fluttering toddler boys had an intense interest in your car seat and toys. One was hovering over you in a particularly persistent way, and though it was apparent he and I had no common language, I realized that he expected to be able to pick you up and hold you. He must have had a baby at home. He grew bored with playing with your toes and wandered off.

Half an hour wait was marked by a larger crowd of families, a growing stack of yellow paper files, and not a doctor in sight. The little boy was back. He was interested in your bottle and my cashews.

I had to listen closely for your African name, as I am not used to the unfamiliar sound of it. A little girl of about twenty months belonged to the only white family in the waiting room. She was on her belly licking the floor. Her brother, about six, had a horribly distended stomach. He spilled a package of chips on the floor.

Two hours' wait and the stack of files was getting precariously higher and higher on the little wooden table next to me. I asked the nurses how long it might take and they seemed almost gleeful to report that the doctors were not yet down from the operating theatres.

The little boy came back carrying a can of Coke. He held out his hand for a sweetie while I was digging in my bag for my pen.

Your surgeon arrived after three-and-a-half hours, saw me sitting with you, remembered who I was, and put your file on top of the now teetering stack.

Once we were alone in the examining room, we chatted professionally about vaginas and perineums, and he related the devastation of the night you came into the emergency unit to be operated on. He said he didn't know what he was stitching—he just stitched and prayed. Alongside him, the nurses and other doctors were all crying while they sewed you up to save your life, to save you from bleeding to death. He took photos of your torn bottom that night, but he refused to show them to me. He examined your bottom, and was pleased. I asked some questions about your care, your medications, the upcoming surgeries.

Your pediatric surgeon introduced me to the hospital's head of pediatrics. Then he asked me to visit him in his private rooms from now on, and assured me that the first repair surgery would be in about eight weeks.

January 15, 2002

BEING A PARENT IS A SACRED GIFT. I think I understand your biomom's anguish at being incapable of taking care of you, perhaps better than almost anyone else could. Having you in my life brings back memories of raising three children alone, and the stinging ostracism and isolation from my family. I remember the shattering grey desperation of being on the streets with two-year-old Juma and Tiba, just a three-day-old infant. I remember the suffocating insecurity and the quiet loneliness. Keeping vigil on my own life like the last sentry on a forsaken, flat, and colorless dusty plain. Your presence has triggered these memories and feelings, and I allow them to wash over me, mingling with and washing away the persistent sadness. Yet never did I, then or now, feel that I could abandon the God-given trust that having responsibility for a child entails. Selfishly, yes, I worried for myself, but I never doubted that I would also take care of the little people who shared my nomadic life.

What was going on in Nomsa's broken life to harden her heart to you? Was it drugs and alcohol? Ignorance? Poverty? A lack of love and care in her own life? No doubt she had experienced some unforgivable abuse, but could it have been severe enough to have left her deaf and blind to your needs like this? My heart goes out to her. If only she could have opened her eyes and seen how beautiful you are. If only she had listened to your cries.

I don't know how to feel about the men who have savaged you. Like wild dogs, they ripped and brutalized you. Right now I feel neither anger nor forgiveness. If I were to have to go to court and see them, I would force myself to simply observe, like a scientist, with curiosity. No, it is not the first time that I have seen the crazily inexplicable face of evil that shows itself as a complete lack of humanity. I saw it too often in Rwanda, Cambodia, Guatemala. I know not to be surprised when these vile actions hide behind the façade of any ordinary man or woman. Yet, when I clean your little bottom, I am reminded that someone hurt my precious baby, and something in me wants them to realize and pay for that hurt with their own tears. Perhaps only their ability to feel remorse, pain, and guilt can bring them back to their humanity. They have Acheron's river, an ocean of tears they must shed, then, before that unlikely shot at redemption.

January 18, 2002

I AM SLOWLY BEGINNING TO READ MORE about child sexual abuse. What else but that our circumstances compel us toward our awareness? Here you are in my life, and here my life intersects with a subject I paid scant attention to in the past. Child abuse I knew about, of course, from all those parenting classes I used to teach as a midwife, making referrals to state social services for troubled new parents—usually single mothers with too many demands and too few resources. The sexual abuse of children? My mind still reels in shock and wonder.

Of course I know about the Virgin Myth. The fact was intricately linked to education in my HIV-prevention programs that Sugar Daddies from all parts of the globe would go after schoolgirls to cure themselves of this disease. Desperate and dangerous men going after suggestible young women who would give away their virginity, and ultimately their lives, for a bucket of popcorn, some new shoes, a cell phone, or a new school notebook. It was almost as hard for us as development workers to convince pubescent girls, hormones and hungers raging, to resist these men as it was to persuade these predatory men that the harm they were inflicting on the innocent was cruel, criminal, and tragically ineffective. Seeking to cure the incurable by raping the bodies and hearts of young women who were unable to perceive the risk or a way to say no to their own deflowering.

The rape of very young girls, of babies, is not something I have come across before, however, and I have been introduced in my reading to Lloyd de Mause, a psychoanalyst and historian who has researched childrearing practices back to antiquity. De Mause concludes that child abuse is the norm rather than the exception, and that young children were often used as "poison containers." "Sexual intercourse with the pure," says de Mause, "was an antidote to the impure."

Dr. de Mause (1993) is emphatic in his description of the Virgin Myth:

> As late as the end of the nineteenth century, men who were brought into Old Bailey (prison) for having raped young girls were let go because "they believed that they were curing themselves of venereal disease." Raping virgins was particularly effective for impotence and depression; as one medical book put it, "Breaking a maiden's seal is one of the best antidotes for one's ills." Thus British doctors in the nineteenth century regularly found when visiting men who had venereal disease that their children also had the same disease—on their mouths, anuses, or genitals.

So it is Dr. de Mause whom I have to thank for providing me with another perspective on the crime against you. I am not sure if the cause of your rape was the belief that it could cure the two alleged perpetrators of HIV. Somehow I doubt it, though. It seems to me this crime against you was less planned, more like senseless, random, impulsive violence against innocence and helplessness. I'll wait with some impatience for your final AIDS test, but ultimately I'm not at all sure it matters to me if an excuse of such supreme ignorance was the reason for your violation.

January 20, 2002

YOU ARE COMFORTABLY INTO A ROUTINE AT HOME. You sleep
ten hours at night, quickly outgrowing your little rattan
basinet, pushing growing feet and head against your beloved
stuffed animals. I have started reading to you—*Peter Rabbit*
and *The Hungry Caterpillar*. You sit quietly in my lap for story
time; you seem to love listening to the musical tones of my
story voice. We sing a few songs and then I put you down
to sleep. You clutch at your blanket, bat your hand at your
chimes, throw your stuffed bunny around, and finally, sucking
your thumb, fall into a deep sleep.

It is your singing and cooing that lets me know when you
are awake. I come into your room to ask about my "Little
Bird" and I am flooded with the bright sunshine of a child's
smile. You then pay attention to the business of devouring
your first bottle of soy formula and afterwards lie quietly
watching the crystal rainbows dance on my bedroom wall,
turning with the early morning breeze. Then you feast on a
breakfast of cereal and fresh fruit. We play and talk and you
go back to sleep for a long nap. Midday you spend hours
awake and active.

You have discovered the leafy joys of riding around our suburban neighborhood in your pram, your eyes playing with the shadow and sunlight as it dances across your little brown legs. You take one long nap before dinner. During the day we manage to fit in a bath, a change of colostomy bag, and, of course, time to pick out a fancy, frilly dress for you to wear.

When you are fussy it usually means you want time to be alone—you like being alone, and do not usually like to be held for sleep. Sometimes you enjoy sitting in your baby chair and watching the dancing of the fairy dust in the sunbeams or watching me bustling about in the kitchen.

I enjoy your routines, and now that I am getting more sleep I am feeling more secure about resuming some of my patiently waiting projects. My old life? Ha, there is no such thing.

We danced in this New Year's Eve, to make sure that we continue dancing all of this year.

January 21, 2002

ONCE UPON A TIME.[3] Once upon a time in a peaceful kingdom, a King and Queen, loving parents, lost their only child—a beautiful little girl. A lonely old woman, who was indeed an old witch, but was not a bad or evil person, took the little Princess from her crib one dark and stormy night. She was just lonely and heartbroken, and desperately wanted a child of her own to love and care for.

So while the King and Queen grieved for years over the loss of their only child, and sent their helpers from one end of the kingdom to the other searching for her, the beautiful little Princess was growing up on a small farm not too far away from them, loved, watched over, and cared for by the old witch who was not her real mother.

Sixteen years passed quickly by, and as it happened, a handsome Prince was passing through the kingdom, seeking adventure and experience, and a young woman to wed. The Prince heard the tale of the Stolen Princess, a story still told around evening fires, and being a wise young man he devised a clever plan to find the Princess in exchange for her hand in marriage, if, once found, she wanted to wed.

And so it began that every night a woman in the kingdom would be invited to spend the night in a special and enchanting hut, where there were music and flowers and twenty downy-soft sleeping mats piled high, one on top of the other. Secretly, however, the Prince, the King, and the Queen had placed an uncooked pea on the center of the first mat on the bottom of the pile. And they waited.

Young women and old, beautiful women and plain, the women of the kingdom waited for weeks to spend a night in the royal house, which each had heard was the most comfortable and luxurious in the land. Every one was given their turn. Finally, when no woman remained waiting, the Stolen Princess, who had heard this fanciful tale, went shyly and curiously to the royal house and asked if she might spend the night before the long walk back to her farm.

All night the Princess tossed and turned, for despite the beautiful surroundings, the music and flowers and fluffy mats, she could never get comfortable. In the morning she graciously thanked the royal family for their hospitality, but being raised to tell the truth she added, "But you must check your sleeping mats, it seems a rock has slipped under them."

The King and Queen began to cry great big tears of joy, the drums played throughout the kingdom, and the dancers and singers declared everywhere that the Lost Princess had been found.

The Prince took the hand of the young woman, related her true story, and then confessed about the hidden pea.

"Only a True Princess is sensitive enough to feel such discomfort," he said. "And you are a True Princess. But the pea is also a reminder that no matter the luxury and comfort of our position as members of the royal family, we must always be sensitive to the misery, discomfort, or unhappiness in our kingdom. Great privilege requires great sensitivity."

And so the beautiful Princess embraced her parents, forgave the woman who raised her, and fell deeply in love with the wise and handsome Prince. And they were married and they all lived happily ever after.

January 23, 2002

YOU HAVE A STEADY STEAM OF VISITORS. What a good baby you are, undemanding, self-comforting, alert, curious, and social. You delight in love kisses, tickles, and music. I am enjoying you, knowing fully well how quickly these special times fly by, and how meaningful it is that you have found a home of love, nurturing, stimulation, acceptance, security, and protection. You are a beautiful, tightly curled rosebud, whose color is as yet unknown.

We had our first fight this morning, over that uniquely bonding, embattling mother-daughter ritual—braiding hair. You were upside down and backwards in protest, pushing, hitting, pulling, and complaining, but somehow I managed to get twelve little multicolored plastic flowers and butterflies on your head. I was exhausted, and you immediately fell into a deep nap, nestled into my smooth cotton sheets as if you never wanted to leave.

Suddenly I was flooded with remembering my mother's hands in my hair. Braiding, twisting, pulling, and plaiting my stiff unruly curls into the signature bows and ribbons of little black girls' hairdos. I hated it as much as you did, but even as a child I knew it was an act of care and love.

Has your mother abandoned you? She came to court to be scolded by the magistrate and to find out that the court was legally removing you from her care. Only time can tell if she can get her priorities straight now. But to be black, single, young, female, uneducated, poor, homeless, and strung out on drugs in the New South Africa? The odds are stacked so heavily against her.

I must confess that I view men quite differently since meeting you. They fall into three categories—the ones who would not even conceive of such a vile act; those who have no brakes on their behavior; and the three men I trust enough to leave you alone in their care—the three I have raised myself. It's not rational, but when I pass men on the streets, I find myself examining each one of them to see if I can tell at a hurried glance which category they fall into. I must admit that I am not very generous; these days most men are looking very suspicious to me.

February 2, 2002

TODAY I TOOK YOU TO WORK WITH ME for the first time. It was hectic chaos to say the least. Perhaps there is nothing that puts a single parent more on edge than the clutching feeling of helplessness at having to look like a career woman and a mother at the same time. It's an impossible task. Fortunately, by this age, my woman's ego is no longer caught up in either career or motherhood. One I do because it comes naturally, the other because I enjoy it, and I have to. Neither role defines who I am, nor do I define myself any longer by these roles. The combination, however, is still overwhelming.

It took an hour to get out of the house. Half an hour to get ready, dressing us both, getting my books and papers, your food and supplies. Then it took half an hour to pack up the car with all of your things—folded cots, prams, diaper bags, and toys. Fortunately you are undemanding, and we know each other well enough by now. Even more fortunately I work in a university, I can close my office door and work on my computer, answering to no one, interacting with few, and not having to watch over my shoulder to see who is looking at the clock when I enter or leave.

You registered your outrage and protest at the new and unfamiliar surroundings, but eventually you fell into a light and fitful sleep in your portable crib, which allowed me to attend to one-fourth of the work I had wanted to accomplish.

I am writing an academic paper about you. I saw an email advertisement for a conference about sex and sexuality, to be held here in Johannesburg, and I decided it was a way to combine my search for answers about the causes and consequences of the crime of infant rape with literature research on my theories about parenting non-violent men.

I need to know. I have the responsibility to know. Unanswered questions burn like pitch in my head and heart, and I realize I cannot come to you with this current turmoil of nagging uncertainty. I plunge into the roiling sea of studies on crime, violence, and masculinity with my intellectual curiosity as a life line. You sit, wide-eyed and quietly, waiting for me on the shores of your imminent womanhood. Well do I know how quickly your true flowering will come.

March 2002

Partial police report: *"I received a rape complaint from the public telephone at the corner of Bok and Twist streets. I arrived a few minutes later and found the mother of the infant who was raped in the company of another female. We then rushed the infant together with the mother to Johannesburg General Hospital and there we contacted the Child Protection Unit while at the hospital because we could not wait at the station and wait for the Child Protection Unit while the baby was in terrible pain."*

THIS STORY IS COMPELLING, horrendous, sickening. What animals could violate and defile an infant girl? Twelve days after the rape this Princess was lying quietly on top of my snowy white cotton blanket, listening to classical music, and watching the rainbows from my crystals dance in the wind. I do realize her life has changed completely. My life has changed completely.

How can I care for this infant with special needs? What lessons of unconditional love, attention, and courage do I need to borrow from my Birth Sisters, my Grandmothers of the Umbilical Cord?[4] Is this enough to heal my infant daughter? Is it sufficient to know that the volcanic pain and blood lava of labor gives birth to joy? Gives light? Dar luz? Does my Mother Wit remind me that our bottoms are designed to rip and tear and heal? But will blood, light, and joy transform this evil act, the trauma and her sacrifice? Will there be a resurrection, and will it blind us or save us all?

As a midwife I am confidently capable of the care of her little bottom, and have begun to give her Rescue Remedy, comfrey tea, and warm olive oil and vitamin E rubs. I am also confident that I can offer her the intellectual stimulation that will accelerate my baby girl's cognitive and emotional healing.

Despite the frustration and tears I have no regrets.

March 1990

WHAT YOU HAVE TO REALIZE about my extended family is that my uncles were an extension of my aunts—May, Bay, and Clarice. Forget about what you have read or think you know about the Moynihan Report and his prescriptions on the Black American Matriarchal Family. You don't know nothin' about us. Aunt May, Aunt Bay, and Aunt Clarice, my grandmother's (Aunt Elsie or Big Sister, depending on where you fell in the order of things) sisters.

They tried to help my uppity mother—Big Sister's only child—raise me not to be as uppity as she was. They failed. Meanwhile they raised me to enjoy family barbeques on humid Saturday afternoons. Potato salad, chocolate cake, chicken fried, smothered and shake-and-baked, apple pie, homemade vanilla ice cream from the churn you couldn't plug in, fresh tomatoes from the garden, fried corn patties with bacon, lemon pound cake, fried apples, collard greens (with fatback until my brother Kojo and I went vegetarian on them), potatoes fried, smothered with onions, hot rolls.

They braided my hair when my mother didn't want to deal with the predictable struggle. They gave me a bath when my mother was at a meeting. They let me play with all the knick-knacks on the shelves when I needed to be entertained and my mother was too busy. They taught me about drinking scotch while playing Bid Whist like a natural Black woman— loud, lots of laughing, lots of testifying.

They showed me by example how to simultaneously take care of a man, children, a home, and a job—a lesson my mother wasn't sure I had ever learned properly. They took in boarders, they adopted and fostered somebody else's unwanted children, and they fed me succotash of corn, lima beans, and tomatoes in the back of restaurants they or one of their daughters were always trying to keep going.

They greased my legs up with Vaseline even though I was too fair-skinned to get as ashy as the other kids. They spanked me, scolded me, hugged me, and praised me. They outlived their niece, Vivian, my mother, every one of them, long enough to find out that I had become more uppity than they had tried their hardest not to allow me to be and less disappointed with my lot in life as a Black woman than my uppity mom.

I am my mother's daughter, every cell of me fed by the moisture drawn through the Virginia soil-embedded roots of her mother's sisters.

April 2002

IT HAS BEEN ALMOST FIVE MONTHS. After a homecoming celebration with an odd group of friends and strangers, and an impromptu Blessingway, during which I sang my favorite Native American birthing songs, much to a little girl's delight, Nolothando has a new name and a new life. Last week she went back to the public hospital for a second repair of her perineum. She had to be put to sleep in the operating room in order for the doctors to be able to fully examine her and see the extent of the healing and remaining damage. The surgeon suspected a number of incompletely joined spots might be present and I had already seen a few thin spots myself. It is miraculous that she has not suffered greater damage, as the original injury was a jagged tear from vagina through anal sphincter.

The surgeon had warned me that if the baby's perineal skin was not strong enough he would have to do a skin graft from her labia, but the months of midwifery care seem to have been sufficient and all Baby Vi needed was a clean cut and stitch back up. By six hours post op she was standing up in her hospital crib, shaking the bars to try to wake up all the other babies in the ward.

She was reassuringly naughty, as only a nine-month-old can be. The pediatric nurses, most of whom already knew and had taken care of her during the dark days of her ordeal, treated her as the Prodigal Daughter—their frustration and rage poured into love and gratitude for the transformed Princess she had become. They warmly teased her about her American accent, fancy hairdo, and up-market baby clothes. They brought me warm corn porridge and blankets as I slept on the hospital floor to try to keep the hordes of roaches from overwhelming her hospital crib that night.

I continue to go to court every month to try to finalize the fostering process. I recognize and understand that this will take time. The birth mother shows up at court but refuses to visit the baby. I do not worry—I recognize my daughter, and remember that in any instance God only gives our children to us as a gift for however long we get that privilege.

Hopefully we have only one more surgery to go—the closing of the colostomy site.

May 2002

Ask, and it shall be given you;
Seek, and ye shall find;
Knock, and it shall be opened unto you.

MATTHEW 7:7

THE WIND SOUNDS LIKE THE DISTANT LAUGHTER of children
on a playground, hop scotching through the trees, cyclical,
shouting and frolicking noisily through the leafy jacaranda trees.

I wrap you and your colostomy bag, not yet full, in a
blanket against the cool afternoon, and I take you out in the
stroller. I am still not used to pushing a pram. It requires
leg and arm muscles that I have not used for some fifteen
years. I amuse myself with how many of the simple tasks of
mothering an infant I have utterly forgotten. Yet, as I push this
beautiful gumdrop-fat baby in her pram I feel inordinately
proud of her, as if her radiance is an extension of me. I want
all the neighborhood domestic workers, the Aunties, to stop
and coo and croon and admire her, which they do. I am taking
in their comments like compliments, sinking in like water on

dry sand. I am ashamed, and greatly entertained, that so small a thing as a child once again tweaks my self-esteem.

I have been having weekly fights with the pediatric surgeons. It is not too soon to examine your perineum for complete healing and to sew up your colostomy site, but I have refused to go back to the public hospital. The dirt, the lack of privacy, the infestation of armies of poison-resistant roaches, the inadequate, understaffed nursing care. The surgeon refuses to operate in a private hospital, even though our pediatrician is prepared to help us have all the fees and costs waived.

I'm outraged by his refusal. And so we continue our now epic battles over principles. The easily assumed overblown sense of entitlement of my American-ness comes crashing to the fore. You are my daughter, you deserve and you will get the best. The surgeon rebuts that you are still a ward of the State—indigent and black. We have screaming matches on the cell phone.

"I'm the doctor! I know what's best for this patient!"

"No! I'm her mother! I know what's best for my child!"

I accuse him of lousy interpersonal skills and racism. He retorts that I am an unfit, overly emotional mother. I am a force of nature, reduced to tears of frustrated, steaming rage. We remain at a stalemate, and I continue to change your colostomy bag every night, not yet knowing your HIV status, not being able to prevent my medical self from looking for obscure signs of seroconversion.

June 2002

On June 10, 2002, the South African Children's Court, housed in an imposing, impossible maze of bureaucratic offices on Market Street, made me Nolothando's official Foster Mother. This comes after five court appearances, each one a welcome endurance test of my commitment, some of them six-hour episodes of sitting on wooden benches in dusty hallways. The magistrates and social workers kept setting new court dates due to the lack of conclusive evidence or information in the investigations of the crime.

Was the State trying to make me prove that I wanted this child through these obscure, ritualized tests of my patience? Then so be it. I stuffed my colorful Guatemalan cotton briefcase with student essays and sat in the hallways, reading and marking papers and unobtrusively observing the in and out drama of family lives caught in the spider's web of the South African judicial system.

Somehow, Nomsa, the birth mother, and I both made it to each court appearance. The third time at court we had lunch together—a tasty homemade curry chicken with rice, dished out from a cardboard box by the corner street vendor, and eaten in companionable silence. The next time at court we had tea together and I tried to get to know her. But she was reticent—a combination of language and respect?

To become a foster mother I had to go to four weeks of parenting classes and five personal interviews at the department of Child Welfare. More hoops to jump willingly through for this much-wanted baby. I had only to remind myself of the reason for all this red tape and I became patient, observing with the eye of an anthropologist.

As a foster mother I don't have to go to court appearances for another two years. I have legal rights, and even the biological mother cannot take the baby from me. If biomom does not show any interest in Nolothando over the next two years, the court can order an adoption. I will take that eventuality one day at a time.

I am outside of my ordered, predictable, middle-class world. My new child's world is a jigsaw of courts and crimes, social workers and police, and family dramas, and it is chaotic, unpredictable.

How dare I? What hubris! Where is this imagined boundary, this Rubicon that I draw across my arrogance and impatience? In accepting my daughter I have wholly taken in this other life I imagine as different, and instead I find only my own distorted image staring back at me from the tarnished silver of this cracked and dusty mirror. I see myself, my life, my fears, my hopes, in the chubby, undimmed sunlight of a baby's smile.

July 2002

I HAVE JUST HEARD THAT THE MEN ACCUSED of your rape have been released from jail. The DNA evidence was inconclusive. The chemicals in your diaper hopelessly contaminated it. I later learned that frantic phone calls were made by the Johannesburg police to forensic labs worldwide to try to correct this error. They were unsuccessful. The men accused of raping you have walked free.

The surgeons, and now the private hospital, continue to play political games with my decisions. It annoys me, but I dig in my heels. No one can understand how difficult it is to get a crawling baby to stay still to change a colostomy bag. Unlike poopy diapers, the feces in the bag is still very alkaline and leaves horrid raw burns on sensitive baby skin if leaks are not cleaned immediately. Sometimes I rush home from work to change the bag with my work skirt, stockings, and high heels still on. I am amazed that you are not getting tired of "The Wheels on the Bus," as I have discovered a multitude of new working parts of buses with which to make verses. I am frustrated but patient. I know what I want.

July 1996

TAKE NO DAY FOR GRANTED

In these truly beautiful tropical places
death blows with carefree abandon
all around us
blustery she can be found
in the faces of young men
hiding behind any bush
death whispers in the eyes of malnourished infants
lying light as feathers in their mother's arms.

At home, litigious Americans have a collective fear
of death and denial of life's risks
unlike anywhere else I have seen
even though no amount of lawsuits or malpractice
    insurance
can protect us from death's arrival,
at her own good time.

To one extent Americans
surround themselves with a false sense of security

from threat and terror
trying to control the uncontrollable,
and the other extreme
societies so traumatized by violence
they think the abnormal is normal
they know nothing else
an equally false sense that life is cheap
almost meaningless in how easily it is surrendered or
    taken.

Life is sacred, fragile
and beyond our absolute control.

Take no day for granted.
Be your soul like a coco palm
bending,
swaying,
responding to the breeze,
yielding
to the strongest wind.

August 10, 2002

WE SPENT ANOTHER NIGHT IN THE HOSPITAL. This time the private hospital where your pediatrician is resident. You somehow managed to catch a bad stomach bug from one of your little friends and within twelve hours the diarrhea draining from your colostomy site was pure water, burning, viscous, and smelly. I woke to your mewing whisper at four in the morning, and held you in my arms for three hours, trying to coax you to drink juice and oral rehydration salts and water, which you kept refusing. I watched as your life force ebbed slowly away until by seven you were too weak to cry, too weak even to hold your head up. I knew from my years of tropical midwifery how quickly a child can dehydrate, but I had no experience of the terror of dehydration through a colostomy.

I bundled you up at seven fifteen and drove fifteen minutes to the pediatrician's office, waiting in the car with you for half an hour until he came. The doctor examined you and agreed with me that you were dangerously dehydrated and required constant monitoring. The Garden City Clinic hospital administrator agreed to waive your costs and fees and we were hurriedly admitted to a pediatric isolation room.

The nurses started an IV on your tiny fist and we attached your colostomy bag to a urine catheter bag to measure and monitor your output of fluids. I sat by your crib, singing to you and coaxing you to drink orange-flavored rehydration fluid out of your bottle. After three children, and never spending a single day in a hospital, not even for their births, I found it harrowing to care for a sick and hospitalized baby.

I have taken so much for granted. I felt insubstantial in my vulnerability. I felt alone and fragile, an insignificant wisp of smoke. I celebrated with a weary sigh when you felt strong enough to crawl around the hospital floor, dragging your tubes and bags along behind you with utter abandon. Your imperative to move and explore was stronger than my self-pity.

August 15, 2002

THE BABY'S NEXT SURGERY IS FINALLY SCHEDULED. Entitled, empowered, pushy mom, yet how many more fights can I have with these doctors? I don't mind really, as I am convinced that I must be a strong and fearless advocate for this child—is that not what she deserves? Is this not why I am her mother? I am thankful that my pediatrician has been supportive of my wish for her not to have her next surgery in the public hospital. Surely my Princess deserves better than that.

How many tears of frustration have I now cried over this damn colostomy bag anyway? I watch her crawling around the house with a bag of poop hanging off her waist and it infuriates me. It is a constant reminder of what has happened to her. And with her being so active there is now no way to keep the bags in place without copious amounts of glue and tape that tear at her sensitive skin when I take them off, leaving red, weeping, bleeding wounds.

Vi is at a delightful age of new tricks and naughtiness every day. She wakes up laughing and goes to bed singing. I consider myself lucky to have recognized an opportunity to do something that December day in Johannesburg Hospital, and to be in a position to say yes. Love was whispering in my ear through the harridan screaming of nameless fears in a moment of recognized serendipity.

August 1997

DEVELOPMENT LESSONS LEARNED

I am willfully disobedient.

You call yourselves leaders
but your moral and intellectual leadership is bankrupt
you are without empathy or compassion
you make a fortune off of the suffering of others.

The real leaders are the men and women
who make magic out of ashes
who survive on hope and stories.

I am wholly unrepentant.

You live a life with no benchmarks
you measure yourself against your own pride
you count your hubris your due, willing to sacrifice
the wombs of young women to your insatiable need
for control.

The fullness of achievement is with those
who yield to a sense of wonder and awe
who understand the ultimate capriciousness of fate.

I challenge your authority.

Your courage lies in squashing any
who are different from your correctness
you are ruthless with a hint of nonconformity
you lift your gin and tonics in five-star hotel bars
to toast those who reflect back your chosen image
you consider yourself a conquering hero, a warrior.

The real bravery is from those
who can face their own helplessness,
who because they know their interdependence with you
can forgive you with their love.

September 2002

Dear Friends, Colleagues, and Family,

I just wanted you all to know that Vi is fine. She was voted out of hospital on Monday night after a successful surgery Saturday afternoon to close her colostomy site. She is acting like a normal toddler, and pretty much as if nothing has happened. The new pediatric surgeon had heard about my reputation as a Pushy American Mom (smile) and after the anesthesiologist let me put the baby to sleep in my arms, the surgeon called me back into the theatre so that we could do the examination of her bottom together. Her bottom has healed completely and to my satisfaction. And her final HIV test was conclusively negative.

Much to the amusement of the pediatric intensive care nurses I spent every hour by her bedside. When she slept I snuck out to eat and shower. Otherwise I was there; I helped change her dressings and give her medicines, and watched to see that she was given the right pain meds. I could tell that my presence was needed when she woke confused or hurting. She clung to my chest, her life line to comfort being found in the familiar warmth and smell of my breasts, the touch of my arms around her, my breath soft against her neck, singing her favorite songs in a slow, deep voice.

I feel that I have so much to be thankful for, and your prayers and good wishes have been an amazing source of support and strength. Thank you so much for thinking of us.

I have learned a great deal these last ten months. Among the most important lessons is that I have been reminded not to ever take for granted the giving and receiving of the hugs and love of my children.

I will rededicate myself to working on behalf of the youngest victims, and to seeing what I personally can do to make sure that this crime against them is brought to a halt.

Much love, Claudia

October 2002

WITH MY EYES SOFTLY SHUT I sit in silence, contemplating the secret language of trees, the sensual curves of the earth. The birds laugh at me, mock my insignificant struggle for inner peace with their glorious, bawdy morning songs. My eyes when open see the clear golden hues of humility and awe.

My arguments with friends have strengthened my resolve. What began as a seed of an idea, nurtured secretly in a bruised heart, and watered by my sorrow and frustration is now pushing away the layers of resistance, the naysayers, the doubts born of my own fears.

I must speak out. I have no choice. I am in a unique position as your mother. I am not encumbered by the dysfunction and disempowerment that usually accompanies these crimes. I have a voice. I can speak—speak with compassion and some measure of wisdom. I can protect your privacy even as I exploit your story.

You are no different from any other little girl, from every other little girl who has suffered from rape and sexual abuse and neglect. I do not want any other parent or any other child to go through the agony of what we have been through. Only my voice, strong, clear, and purposeful, will stop this screaming in my ears.

November 2001

Why the baby hungry again?

She so little.

She want suck too much.

No time.

No milk.

Powder milk keep her quiet.

Get enough coins buy a bag of powder.

Mix it some water.

Now she crying again.

Wet again.

Hungry again.

Slap her.

She whimper.

Suck finger.

Sleep.

I come right back.

Have to find something.

For her.

For me.

December 2002

Pies, para qué los quiero
Si tengo alas pa'volar.

FRIDA KAHLO, 1953

(Why do I need feet when I have wings to fly?)

OTHER THAN MY DAILY SOJOURNS TO MY OFFICE at the university, and cameo appearances in the queues of the South African bureaucracy, this is the first time I am venturing out without you. How appropriate that my escape from the tentacles of mothering have led me to the theatre to see the new movie, *Frida*.

I openly weep at her violent accidental impaling and it becomes yours, and I cry out for her pain and it is your pain I am crying for. Will twinning plants, roots, and veins grow from your violated body? Will the blood of your deflowering spill over you like tears of love and flow like bath water from your bruised and exposed heart? Blood has stained your innocence like Frida's white lace Victorian dress.

Your mother has turned away, deserted you. Left you like a broken china doll, a broken imperfect toy. She is petulant; what bruised and hidden pain has wrenched her heart from her, impaling an empty space and leaving her womb open but dry, a decaying flower bud that will never fully bloom?

Is my love for you, my little dove, enough to heal this wounding? Why rape? Why is your rite of passage and pain so violently and intimately extricated with the chalice of your very being? Am I the sage femme, enough of an Earth Mother to nourish your opened and broken body to a woman's wholeness at my breasts? Can the aorta of my love entwine the dendrites that have grown out of your pain and heal the nightmares of your inner life?

Or will you be like Frida, herself a July-born child, gracing us with her immense talent, while forcing us to look into the mirror of our lives and see the blood we reap and the pain we sow amidst the shards of a beautiful legacy of strength?

Frida died the year I was born. And too, my little one, I died and was reborn in the blood of your ordeal. From my mouth I spit out anger and sorrow like watermelon seeds, and I return home, at peace, to the tasks of taking care of you.

> "Frida, who was not at first aware of what had happened, thought only of retrieving the second toy she had lost that day but was unable to do anything. There she lay like a broken china doll, covered with blood and gold dust, which apparently another passenger had been carrying. Frida heard someone shout 'La bailarinita, la bailarinita!' Her fellow-passengers thought this pale creature dusted with gold was a ballerina."

FROM ALCÁNTARA AND EGNOLFF,
FRIDA KAHLO AND DIEGO RIVERA, PRESTEL, 2001.[5]

January 2003

IN SPEAKING OUT I have found that many listen with shocked ears or read through their tears, and they want to reach out. They want to talk, to ask questions, and they want to help. I have gathered together a small group of friends and started a trust in honor of my daughter—The Princess Trust. After only three meetings we ran smack up against the central issue—is this about Vyanna or is it about the rape of South Africa's children?

I am clear in my mind—it is about both. Others are not clear. Some of my board members have retreated, withdrawn their assistance. Some have said there is a need to protect Vyanna that extends to making up stories about her injuries. I accept their concern out of compassion, but they are wrong. My daughter is not to blame for what happened to her. There is no shame, no stain on her soul, no scarlet letter that she must pin to her chest. She will always know that this horrid crime is not who she is—it is just a thread in the tapestry of her as yet unfinished story.

Dear Board Members,

I want to do what is best for my daughter, and I include in that the passion to do something about the very issues she has had to face. I honestly don't put her or myself in any position of importance or superiority greater than that of the other mothers and babies who have been and are going through what we have been and are going through. The real difference lies in the responsibility on my shoulders for my inherited and earned privileges. I *don't* put those responsibilities on the shoulders of a seventeen-month-old, certainly that would be stupid and irresponsible of me. But I do take those responsibilities on myself seriously. I am not asking that you take on those responsibilities. I am also not asking that you understand my sense of duty or my reasons for speaking out. I would love to ask that you accept that I have made an informed, thoughtful decision and not try to beat me up with your point of view or opinions. If I have your approval and support, I will treasure it. If I don't have it, I will keep marching right along.

With love, Claudia

March 2003

IT IS A GREAT SELF-REVELATION to know that I can unbundle
my depressions at last. Depression is no longer conjoined
with despair, poverty, and crushing abandonment. This
uncoupling does not ridicule my difficult and oddball past.
Rather it gives to the abyss and the darkness the respect of
place and time that only history accords event. Consigning
my own pain to the fabric softener of history is an act of self-
acknowledgment and respect. I nod to that particular wash
cycle that is completed.

But I have not come out a crisp, clean, and freshly pressed
garment. No amount of starch or bleach can now hide the
faded softness, the rents and shredded seams, the stitching
come apart, the shapelessness. I am a soft rag, struggling to
re-fabricate the epic narratives of my own life.

THEY sit in a circle around a large but low burning
and hot fire. THEY struggle to hide looks of shame, anger,
grief, bewilderment, and compassion behind façade faces
of nonchalance, fake amusement, normalcy. THEY reek of
poisonous confusion and sit like limp curdles of disapproval
and judgment. THEY pointedly ignore me circling briefly

around the outside edges of that non-space between the cold darkness and the warmth, with a small child in my arms. Imperceptibly, THEY draw closer to each other. THEY tighten the circle. THEY take away that which greedily feeds on the twigs and logs of the family. THEY give me cold open space, time, and freedom. THEY consign me forever to that which seeks darkness and shies away from family fires, a wandering life finding warmth only in the small feel of carried bundles.

I endure through the possibilities of horizons and borderlessness and tiny blankets wrapped around warm sweetness. I grow wings of steel and fly hard, often and fast up into the Milky Way. My two hands, head, and feet become the four corners of the Southern Cross. THEY sat in their circle with their backs to me and thought me shamed, banished, and dead.

April 2003

I SPENT MY MOST RECENT SATURDAY AFTERNOON, a typically sunny Johannesburg Saturday, on an agonizing pilgrimage of the heart. A difficult and required journey to the place where my beloved daughter spent the first five months of her life. This was my sojourn to visually assess the place I had imagined since first taking this damaged infant in my arms at the hospital. The exact coordinates of the crime against her, the place where she was brutally raped at such an unimaginably young age.

As so often with such grim but necessary pilgrimages, I was left speechless by the harsh reality of her victimhood. I was left, in that bottomless black pool, once again, without words. I was struggling in my mind to retrace the steps of her mother, the perpetrators of the crime, the phone call with a screaming, bleeding infant in arms. It was worse than I imagined, far worse. How can I capture the sense of horror, outrage, humility, and awe that now fills me?

I met the Chief Inspector of the Child Protection Unit while taping a TV talk show about child sexual abuse. He came up to me after the show, a small, electric, older white man. He introduced himself and told me he had supervised the prosecution of our case. It was he for whom we had waited that first day, for he had to personally give permission for me to take the baby from the hospital and into my home as a place of safety ten days after the incident.

He left me amazed by apologizing that he had not kept in better touch with me, and that I was not properly informed about the legal details of the case.

"You need to know what happened. She needs to know what happened. I'll do anything to help you understand how hard this case has been for us as a police unit. Thank you for taking her in."

I was left speechless by his clarity, humility, and expression of appreciation. We spoke for another fifteen minutes about some details of the case, and then I asked if it was possible to see the hotel—a request he did not hesitate to accept, in fact he encouraged it.

I prepared myself for the visit to the Action Cinema much the same way I prepared myself for my tours of the genocide museum in Phnom Penh, or the births in the Rwandan camps, or visits to new mothers in the slums of Dhaka—I figured, wrongly, that I could handle my shock and grief at witnessing others' raw traumas. It was far worse than I imagined.

The inspector met us in front of the police station and I expected he would be alone on a Saturday afternoon. Instead, he had arranged a police escort of four of his deputies, visibly and heavily armed, including a wiry fellow with an AK47 and two policewomen.

"I never go into this part of Johannesburg alone," he joked.

It began to rain on the way into town. I rode in the back of one of the unmarked police cars. The Action Cinema is still functioning, a ghetto porn theatre, with eight theatres, seven of them roughly boarded up, a receptionist at the ticket window, and a concession stand in the lobby, amidst broken doors and torn seats strewn haphazardly. The theatre was showing porn films twenty-four hours a day.

The Action Cinema. The glass on most of the front doors is cracked. As if some drunk, drug-addled, hyper-stimulated patron has shoved, kicked, and pummeled the panes into intricate glass spider webs, nonsensical treasure maps of anger and violence. Where is the manger?

Our police escort took wide-legged and alert stances, clips off their numerous weapons, conversing with an assortment of patrons and local hang-abouts. A small crowd of men was warily gathering for the two o'clock showing. No one was surprised to see the police in this part of town, in fact the inspector made jokes about being chased away a few times as he zipped up his blue nylon police jacket over his T-shirt and we went toward one of the boarded-up theatres.

We stepped over ankle-deep piles of filth, garbage, rags, and human excrement to get a glimpse of the doorway that led into the place where the crime had taken place. Office cubicle partitions had been fitted into the theatre, cement slabs thrown over the seats and steps to create a bed in each of the six cubicles. The women who lived there were prostitutes, able to rent a room for 20 Rand ($3.50) per night. The sex workers would make enough money early enough to pay for their room and booze and then spend the rest of the day drowning their sorrows.

On December 2, 2001, there were no other children living in the Action Cinema.

In involuntarily hushed voices we talked a bit, and my documentary crew filmed an interview with the inspector. I was unable to stop looking at the public pay phone next to the food stall, trying to imagine the desperation of a young mother bringing a newborn into these horrible conditions. I stood in silent observation, in mute denial. My unshed tears had turned me into a pillar of salt—Lot's wife.[6]

Vyanna, that you survived five months in such squalor and misery is a miracle. A manger of straw is a palace compared to the Action Cinema. Your humble beginnings are as bad as it gets, anywhere, for any child born into extreme poverty and chaos.

This explains the wide-eyed, traumatized, insecure little girl I took into my home in December 2001. What remains a mystery is the vibrant, fearless, charismatic Princess that now gleefully terrorizes us with her toddler antics, and mesmerizes us with her dancing, singing, and free-spirited independence.

We are all blessed to have this particular child among us to care for.

May 2003

INTRODUCTION TO SEX AND SECRECY
CONFERENCE PAPER, JOHANNESBURG,
WITS UNIVERSITY[7]

THE HEINOUS CRIME OF CHILD RAPE SHOCKS US as no other. The recent spate of highly profiled infant-rape cases in South Africa has galvanized us to undergo a more thorough and extremely painful search—through the discourses of psychology, social theory, criminology, and politics, and by examining the social politics of HIV/AIDS, and the issues of gender, power, and violence. The result has been an increase of studies and a cacophony of voices. Now, it is this author's feeble attempt not to add to the din, but only to contribute in a small way to answering that question—whispered or shouted—WHY? Why do (mostly) men rape infants (defined here as under two years of age), mostly girls? This paper— which should be properly called an exploration—attempts an answer by simultaneously looking at an under-explored area of research—the role and importance of parenting, especially of boys, and by asserting the power of constructing a cultural and personal narrative about the rape of a five-month-old infant within an academic text.

Let me begin by declaring my incompetence, not in the usual attempts at academic hubris disguised by protestations of inadequacy and feigned ignorance, but for the purposes of a real disclosure of my lack of academic authority on the subject of infant rape. I'm not a sociologist. I'm not a psychologist, I'm not a criminologist, and I'm not an anthropologist. I'm just a mom.

By training I'm a biologist, by profession I'm a midwife, by career I'm an international development specialist. I'm studying for a doctorate in economics at Wits, and I lecture and practice in rural and urban business economics. I'm a Renaissance woman. A highly educated, First Nations and African American woman, born and raised in the Bronx, transplanted to South Africa by way of the rest of the world. My passion remains with the concerns, fears, and aspirations of women, and with my four children, and at core—I'm just a mom.

Why are these attributes part of this exploration of infant rape or part of my disclaimer about my suitability to be speaking on the subject? Because it was as just a mom that I found myself the caretaker of a five-month-old South African girl who had, eleven days before she found herself a part of my household, been brutally raped here in Johannesburg. And it was my personal exploration of her trauma and my task in healing her that led me to this line of research.

In the midst of the antiretrovirals, the colostomy bags, the hospitalizations, the arguments with the pediatric surgeons,

the care of her torn perineum and her wounded spirit, I
spent months on the internet, in email conversations with
the world's true academically and professionally defined
authorities on infant trauma, and on international message
boards with the parents of emotionally or physically
vulnerable children. I began to search for and read journal
articles. (And we all know when an academic starts reading
journal articles a paper has been thus impregnated.)

I undertook this search for a number of reasons. First, the
effort at research was a natural vehicle for an intellectual to
heal her own trauma of the rape of her daughter—for the
instant I took this baby girl into my arms she was and always
will be as much my child as if I had given birth to her.

Second, this research was my way of rising to the challenge
that was issued by the first question that came to the lips
of every person who met us in those initial few months—
WHY?

As well, this exploration was my attempt to rationalize
the emotional reactions of my three adult sons—all of whom
have reached sexual maturity—the oldest of whom, now at
age twenty-eight, was physically ill when he was told of the
particular cabbage leaf under which his new sister had been
found. How could I dare to be 99.99 percent sure that I had
raised three men who would not even dream of defiling an
infant girl, even as the very fact of my outrage in those early
days was a heightened suspicion of all men, ALL MEN. What
had I done, as a single working mother, to raise non-violent,

non-predatory, non-impulsive men, especially against all the sociological odds within my strange family that is definitively categorized as "other," " non traditional," "not intact," and even "pathological" in all mainstream social and psychological treatises about the family?

However, the fundamental reason for this exploration is that I immediately realized that in taking on the care and healing of this bruised little girl, I was also taking on the responsibility to answer *her* when she asked that question— WHY? Her courage demanded my thoroughness. My hubris is in sharing what I am learning, what I suspect, and what I am hypothesizing with all of you today. Thank you for putting up with this—I hope it adds something to your understanding of the subject of infant rape. And because I am just a mom I also hope it adds something to the resolution of this issue of raising non-violent men, and in seeing that no other parent has to face the tragedy of healing a raped child.

My interests, and the following observations of my research, focus on raising non-violent men. Therefore, I am attempting to deconstruct violent masculinity—predatory and impulsive. I will begin by clarifying my definitions. I will then look at the issues of parenting and infant rape—especially the virgin myth—from a psychohistorical perspective. I will briefly look at the functionality of masculinity and an examination of the neurobiology of violence and trauma. I will end with some comments on parenting as an exercise in intergenerational transformation.

What does it mean to be "a man"? It is my contention, supported by a considerable body of lived experience and research, that current constructs of masculinity are based on the subordination of women and children, with violence and aggression seen as appropriate vehicles to maintain that subordination. There remain widespread norms of the need to dominate, the need to have "strictly male" spheres of control, and the sexualization of women, portrayed as simultaneously weak and emasculating. This construct has become increasingly dysfunctional in an evolved and "modern" world.

The dysfunctionality of masculinity is a complex issue. On one hand, men's economic power, imperative to impregnate, and the need to defend through superior physical strength continue to be accepted and created by both men and women, thereby reinforcing the stereotypic constructs.

On the other hand, male violence is rending the social and emotional fabric of all communities. While not taking a deterministic view that the structures of patriarchy and capitalism "cause" behavior, I do maintain that the social context of the individual and family allows reference points for identity formation, and men construct notions of masculinity by choice. The degree to which any individual man buys into these global ideologies varies by the extent to which they are internally impelled to conform to or rebel against context.

We are aware that when masculinity is linked by social norms and a powerful media industry to sexual prowess or economic success, it is difficult to foster identity formation that rejects violence and aggression in men.

Transforming dysfunctional patterns of aggression requires almost heroic acts of agency on the part of individual men in creating new ideologies of masculinity and individual parents in the discouragement of aggression in their male children. Either of these achievements must take place in the face of overwhelming positive community and media reinforcement for rewarding and maintaining male stereotypes.

I reject the argument that poverty is a cause of crime and violence—it is a correlate not a determinant.

The crisis in masculinity is good news. That male identity formation is undergoing transformation and is currently quite fragile is a hopeful sign. This leaves open the door for a redefinition of roles and norms and the reinforcement of adaptive instead of maladaptive behaviors and traits. In many respects this paper is an attempt to answer the question: "What is the role of heterosexual women in recasting male identities?"

I envision the potential for parenting to be transformative, as the withdrawal of rewards for violence and toughness in sons (or the rewarding of emotionality and vulnerability) creates valuable reinforcement of non-violent masculinity. We are challenged to teach our sons that notions of responsibility and care define the construct of masculinity, and that the modern cultural diet of consumerism and violence works by creating and reinforcing dangerous personal and social insecurity. This requires no less than revisioning the responsibilities and privileges that define masculinity.

Ultimately, in constructing a narrative around the rape of my five-month-old South African daughter I have chosen to become conversant with my multiple roles as mother, mentor, midwife, and therapist. I have consciously chosen a feminist social-work practice as the framework within which to live this narrative with my daughter. I refer to Wood and Roche's (2001) description of feminist social-work practice, especially understanding and modifying for our own requirements the following central principles:

1. Rape inflicts brute violence, and attributes blame, resulting in a silencing of the voice of survivors. A refusal to accept blame or shame is critical to providing the space for a pre-verbal child to find her own voice or silence on this issue.

2. It is not necessary for survivors to retrieve or relive the pain and horror of their experience, but it is essential that they take back their right to interpret that experience.

3. Along with the personal care and healing comes an obligation to undermine oppressive beliefs and the "pervasive cultural discourse about gender that devalues, blames, and subjugates women and girls." That violence in the home

and on the streets are local versions of broader oppressive texts and myths that serve to control women's behavior (Wood and Roche, 2001).

4. That refusing shame and silence is an essential component of honoring my daughter's courage and heroism.

De Mause (1993) posits, "When mothers love and support particularly their daughters, a series of generations can develop new childrearing practices that grow completely new neural networks, hormonal systems, and behavioral traits." Given that traits of masculinity show a more stubborn resistance to change, I would extend this plea to the love and support of our sons.

I should also now declare that this research is in a highly unfinished state, and is definitely an ongoing literature review. This is not empirical research, except perhaps in the ways that, as a feminist single mother, I have experimented on my own sons for the last three decades.

June 2003

AT WHAT COST THIS WISDOM? It stings the eyes like an onion cut too quickly. Wisdom is the odor of sulfur and unwashed eight-year-old child soldiers in my lungs; it sears my alveoli as I struggle to keep my heart beating. It is the wisdom of layers, peeled back one by one, of death and decay and rebirth. It is as if I am blinded in order to sharpen my hearing. I hear the colors of silence. I am silent. I am the silence. I speak into the silence.

July 2003

ONCE UPON A TIME, there was a Real Princess. Beautiful
and beloved by many, she was scorned and mistreated by
her own husband and his royal family. The Real Princess
was touched by the plight of ordinary people, and she was
especially sensitive to war orphans and maimed children. She
tried to teach her own sons the principle of the pea under
the mattress, but we don't yet know if she was successful,
because she died or was killed, a horrible death, while she
was still young. And no one lived happily ever after.

You and Princess Di share a birth date. July first. I
celebrate your life, your courage. Your awesome strength and
fearless courage.

I am about to face the courts again. It is time to present
the magistrate with a petition for your adoption. I am curious
and not scared. Nothing could take me away from being a
part of your life.

August 1988

SOMEDAY OVER TEA

Dear Mom,

IT HAS OCCURRED TO ME that you must often find times to wonder what it is your grown and only daughter is up to—flying your precious grandchildren to far-flung places in dusty corners of the world, or leaving them in one remote country while traveling alone to another. Certainly this has forced you, at least, to consult your atlas a few times, as I imagine you need to spend some time explaining where I am, to those who ask, before you can tackle why.

I know I haven't written to you nearly enough over the years of my adult wanderings, and although I sense you understand what it is I'm "up to" I thought it might help you to hear it from me. It helps me to explain it to you. To sort out the cacophony of memories that follows when one has lived in twenty-three different houses, in twelve different countries, been homeless three times, and is in the "middle" of raising three children. It creates some harmony of my recollections.

By now I figure I have either made a career out my inability to "settle down" or professionalized my proclivity to "run away."

I say that to make you smile. Surely you are remembering a round-faced stubborn-mouthed four-year-old girl with stubby braids, who, completely annoyed with the capriciousness of adult whim, and pouting, would open any dresser drawer, stuff the contents into a pink plastic doll-clothes suitcase, grab a few copper coins, and exit with a deep and mumbled, "I'm running away."

"Where are you going, Claudia?" you asked, genuinely concerned.

"Chicago." I replied, short, and equally mumbled.

Resolutely I would walk down the stairs and close the heavy wooden door behind me. You had the presence of mind to let me go, and to send my big brother out of the door to follow me as I walked around the corner of our street in The Bronx.

I knew he was there, and I walked until my will was overcome by the thought of the hot chocolate and hugs that I knew were waiting for me upstairs in that apartment on 221st Street, when I found my way home.

Dear Mom,

My friends say I lead an interesting life. Yes, that this is true cannot be disputed. I'm here in Panama, the land where a confused sun rises over the Pacific and sets over the Atlantic. To understand you must consult your atlas again.

Portobelo, which you will know translates from Spanish to "beautiful port," is a quaint little town. Nested within the stone ruins of its original Spanish inhabitants, it sleeps on one side of a calm bay. It is beautiful in its tropical simplicity and the sensuousness of the glowing black faces of the local people.

Panama is more developed than where I have been lately. Still, this little fishing village fringed with palms and caressed with the thick fresh salt breezes of the sea has the signs of Third World poverty I have seen everywhere. Amid patchwork wood-plank houses crowded together in muddy fields where families live in two or three rooms covered by zinc sheet roofs, poverty, in Portobelo, is kind.

You can live from the sea, if you make enough money for rice and bread. Fruit is abundant and cheap. The children grow up strong and free, barefoot, scantily clad; the boys are allowed to roam without responsibilities, the girls are protected and their labor is expected at home.

There is no poverty of spirit here; these are a deeply religious people whose town is the home of the famous Black Christ, a symbol of religious piety that even now sees the faithful making pilgrimages, crawling on bleeding and bandaged knees from all over Latin America to *La Iglesia del Cristo Negro de Portobelo*.

I sat in the empty church early this morning, meditating on a simple wooden bench, sitting beneath the cavernous stone ceiling, and admiring the rich tapestries and the many images of *La Virgen*. I recalled so many churches, temples, and mosques where the supplicants cannot sit as I did, in quiet reflection. They cower, instead, at the fulmination of bullets and bombs, within and without the walls of their violated lives and sanctuaries.

This strikes me as a situation of stupendous disorder. How is it that places of worship cannot be free from violence, so that those who come to rest their souls from the battering of intolerance and hatred can converse with the Most High in peace? If peace cannot be found in the abodes of spiritual nourishment, then where will this insanity of strife and war end?

My wanderings have taken me to a few such desperate places. Where the threat of violence hangs over the spirits of the people with relentless daily certainty, like the liquid air of a tropical afternoon. I am amazed at the strength of my hosts and friends, who live under this dank, unmoving cloud. I am awed by their tired fear, compelling them to live a life as close as possible to normal, in their eyes the hope of tranquility, and around their mouths the weary lines of resignation.

Dear Mom,

What a sheltered and peaceful existence you provided for me in childhood. How protected and nurtured my intellectual curiosity and spiritual growth. Is this what draws me to seek over and again the experience of uncertainty within which most people survive?

I remember that in The Bronx I always turned around and came back home. It wasn't fear of the shadows between alleys, of the uncertainty of destination or plans that turned me around to face the protective and questioning gaze of my brother, and trudge silently back up the brick steps to the porch of our modest duplex. I had no sense of failure or loss, simply the knowledge that the adventure had come to its end.

What you provided me with, in infancy and childhood, was the freedom to exercise my will within the structured limits of discipline and the sure knowledge of your love and peace.

I am sitting in a porch hammock in a two-storied wood-framed house watching the shadows of twilight fall softly across the bay and five of Portobelo's children stringing Christmas lights in the branches of an acacia tree, tiny twinkling bulbs the colors of their dreams. Someday soon, Mom, over tea, we must compare notes, of a childhood I remember in such vivid detail.

Dear Mom,

In the mornings the air is cool, a stimulating sensual breeze refreshes the day, washes it free of yesterday's heat and longings, after a night of rain. This morning my artist friend and traveling companion is teaching Maria and her oldest son to make T-shirts. Maria, smelling of the morning's kitchen chores, of wood smoke and coconut oil, is cutting out stencils with a scalpel. Together we will splash colored paint over these stencils onto white shirts. Maria will sell them to the many tourists who pass through the village in the season of piety.

I came for vacation, to relax, write, and read, to fuel the creativity of my hosts, to leave them with the power to make their dreams into strings of tiny colored lights. Empowerment is a strong word, a potent idea, a force that compels me from one experience to another. It is something you taught me about by example through the security of my childhood.

Someday soon, Mom, over tea, we must compare notes.

August 2003

Magistrate and Commissioner
Johannesburg Children's Court
15 Market Street
Johannesburg

Honorable Sir or Madam:

I AM WRITING THIS LETTER TO SUPPORT MY PETITION for the adoption of a South African child, Nolothando Thabede.

On December 10, 2001, I met Nolothando at Johannesburg General Hospital where she was recovering from surgery after being brutally raped on December 2, as she had just completed five months of age. By December 13, Nolothando was in my home, at first as a Place of Safety, and by June 10, 2002 as a Foster Child placement through the Johannesburg Child Welfare Society.

It was at that first meeting, however, that Nolothando found a place in my heart, a place that has only expanded with the joy that she has brought to our family. I must say that the first year was a challenge. Taking on the care of baby Nolothando entailed a month of four-hourly administration of antiretroviral medications, three hospitalizations, the care of an infant colostomy bag for ten months, waiting for the final HIV test, sleepless nights, and the emotional nurturing of a traumatized and neglected infant—these were enormous challenges. I can only say that I am glad that I found the strength to meet these difficulties, and that I have never once regretted my decision to create a place of love and security for this child who I now consider my true daughter.

As an experienced parent I know well that the challenges of raising Nolothando will continue for many years to come. I would in any case be a permanent part of Nolothando's life, but I am requesting that the court look favorably on my desire to adopt Nolothando. I am prepared to raise her as a responsible and secure South African citizen, as I have every intention of remaining in my adopted country on a permanent basis. I will also find great joy in sharing her culture and heritage with her, as I, too, continue to learn about the richness of this great republic.

Finally, however, my heartfelt desire for this adoption lies only in the fact that I love this young child as my own, and feel sure that I can provide Nolothando with the home environment she needs to turn the tragedy of her early life into many years of security and happiness. Thank your for allowing me such an opportunity and privilege.

Respectfully yours,

Claudia J. Ford

September 1, 2003

Dear Friends and Family:

CLOSURE HAS COME to a difficult, challenging, and
totally joyous time in our lives. Hospitalizations, surgeries,
medications, court appearances, interviews with social
workers, police reports—this first phase can now be
celebrated with the completed submission of the official
adoption papers for The Princess to be recognized as what
she has already become—an inseparable part of the Ford
Family. You have all played an important role in supporting and
facilitating the last twenty months and for that we offer our
sincere thanks and appreciation. The Creator's peace and love
for you and yours, Claudia, Juma, Tiba, Tai, and Vyanna Ford.

September 9, 2003

THE MAGISTRATE OF CHILDREN'S COURT Johannesburg at
nine thirty-five a.m. this morning told me, "Nolothando is
now as much yours as if you had given birth to her!" Hooray,
hooray, hooray!!!!

It was almost comical to sit in chambers, feeling like a
naughty school child, taking turns with my social worker to
quietly answer questions about the mother's whereabouts
(unknown). The judge wrote sixteen pages of notes in twenty
minutes, ending with furious stamping and signatures the
repercussions of which I had no idea, and I could only hold
on to the thinnest thread of hope, my mouth dry, my heart
beating wildly. When she finally put down her pen, this
middle-aged auntie, with awesome power over the happiness
of my family, looked at me rather sternly over her glasses
and read the formal language of the court declaring that the
biological mother had abandoned the child and my right to
adopt her.

An impossible smile was seen to tilt the corners of her
mouth, just barely, but there it was. She said I was the most
impressive mother she had seen fit to grant a child to in many
years, that she was thrilled that I had taken on the care of this

particular child, and that Nolothando was now mine as if I had given birth to her. I burst out in tears in the courtroom and the magistrate and social worker finally laughed out loud.

"I'm glad," said the judge with a grin. "I would have been worried if you did not cry."

I don't mind being teased, I know now a rare moment of pure joy, and I cannot wait to scoop you up in my arms, even though you will be totally unaware of the different status of our relationship when you plant that wet, sloppy kiss on my check.

I am once again reduced to wordlessness.

October 1977

I WAS TWO-AND-A-HALF WEEKS, seventeen days, past the due
date for the delivery of my second child. Over a twenty-
four-hour period the ripe watermelon of my ever-expanding
stomach had sprouted a road map of new stretch marks. I
had come down out of the hills in the far north of the state
of Oregon where I was hiding for two months with my active
two-year-old son in a log cabin in the woods on the site of a
deserted scout camp. Lonely redwoods, achingly beautiful,
with no electricity and no running water, I filled the last days
of the short northwestern summer with the soothing chores of
mothering, cooking, and running to the icy stream while Juma
napped, to wash dishes and clothes and draw water for a bath.

My sun-dappled refuge was perched on top of a small
riverbank, water skipping down out of the far distant
mountains pure, cold. and clear, singing over pebbles and
stones. The one-room wood cabin was built on two levels,
with a brick fireplace that doubled as a kitchen hearth, where
warmth and pots of split pea soup and brown rice were
always ready next to a Chinese porcelain teakettle full of
Red Raspberry herb tea. A worn orange bean bag served as
a chair to read bedtime stories and a wooden ladder led up

to a simple sleeping platform where my son and I shared the cold dark nights huddled together under an opened sleeping bag that had old-fashioned hunting prints of ducks on the soft forest green fabric.

As an apprentice midwife I had already delivered a dozen or so babies for other women, so although I was late in my ninth month of pregnancy I did not worry about going into labor alone in the silent woods with only a young child as a companion. I carried my complete birthing kit with me. I was twenty-three years old, but already the two strands of my life were as tightly woven as a simple basket. Isolation and escape. Retreat and flight. Hiding and running away.

One morning I woke from a dreamless sleep and I simply decided that I needed more support as the single mother of two young children than could be found in my forest retreat. I couldn't figure out how to make it on my own through the long, dark, snowy Oregon winter, so I packed my two-year-old, our sleeping bag, and our few pots and pans into a 1968 gold Oldsmobile—a V12 engine having earned it the nickname "The Boat"—and drove south to California, to give birth at my mother's house in Sacramento. Clean, sterile, boring Sacramento of shopping malls and strip malls and car dealerships.

Twenty days overdue, heavily pregnant, and feeling ephemeral and disconnected, I spent the whole day in and out of my mother's bathroom after swallowing a large dose of castor oil to irritate my digestive system and get my contractions going. It failed.

Day twenty-one, Sunday morning, Gail, my midwife and a sister midwifery student, drove from Oakland to Sacramento to do a prenatal check on me and the baby.

"Okay Claudia, why do you think you aren't ready to give birth?" Gail gently asked me in that simple, authoritarian way that midwives acquire.

"My mother's very unhappy. She's unhappy I'm having another child. She's disapproving that I'm not married. She's uncomfortable and unhappy that I'm staying here with her."

"So," directed Gail, "you need to move someplace else so you can give birth."

That same slow ubiquitously sunny California Sunday afternoon I drove to Berkeley in the Oldsmobile to stay at a friend's house.

Monday afternoon I spent walking energetically around a city I had come to enjoy as a summer student. North I walked toward the heavily treed university, up Telegraph Avenue past tables of students and faculty sitting in steamy coffee shops, east past dorms and bookstores with posters of old authors and new books, south down College Avenue past familiar vegetarian restaurants; I walked with the slow, lumbering, dreamy gait of a woman in full sail of pregnancy. That evening as the air cooled, I stopped to reward myself with a slice of chocolate cake, and under my long patchwork quilt skirt my waters dribbled on the floor of the café as I stood at the cash register to pay.

By late Monday night my waters broke as I was stepping out of a warm bath, I went into labor, and not wasting any time on anything but total concentration on my contractions I gave birth an hour-and-a-half later. I delivered a beautiful, healthy baby boy at one twenty a.m. on a Tuesday morning in October in the bedroom of my friend's house. The labor was so fast that my mother, who drove down from Sacramento as soon as I called her, missed the birth. She arrived to find me sitting in bed, The Madonna, holding her second grandson in my arms. A fawn-colored rosebud of a baby boy with an angel's kiss in the shape of a perfect red heart on his right cheek.

Thursday morning I woke and dressed and fed all three of us quite early, gathered dirty clothes for myself, the baby, and the toddler, and prepared to walk three blocks to the public laundromat to do the wash.

While organizing myself to get out of the door of the house my friend's husband stopped me and said, "You and the kids will have to leave by tomorrow."

Two days after childbirth the only thing I can clearly remember is breastfeeding, changing diapers, and gently chastising Juma who was gleefully running up and down the aisles of the laundromat, only barely aware of his new status as a big brother.

Friday, another sunny morning, I packed our suitcase, put Juma in a fold-up stroller I had borrowed from Gail, packed my newborn son into a blue denim front-pouch carrier and walked slowly up Ward Street to the Avenue on one of those cloudless, icicle-blue Bay Area mornings. Mindlessly I passed the neatly tended gardens, low fences, and colorfully painted houses of Berkeley, curtains at bay windows left open on empty scenes of neat domesticity.

I stopped under the shade of a tree on a quiet side street and took quick stock of my situation. I had two very young children, twenty dollars, and no place to sleep other than an old car. I did a rapid mental checklist—my father and brother were barely on speaking terms with me. My mother had already put me out. I had no money and no place to go to sleep and take care of my three-day-old infant and my toddler.

I walked contemplatively a few blocks further, the bright day mocking my situation, and found the Berkeley Women's Health Center, converted from an old house. I went in and sat down at the receptionist's desk, and said, "I'm not sure I can figure out how to take care of these children. I've just given birth, I have no money, and I'm homeless."

The young woman behind the desk quickly assessed me and the children with a look, and with little more than a nod she left the desk to confer with her colleagues and to find a sandwich in the clinic fridge. While breastfeeding I shared the tuna sandwich with Juma and the receptionist made phone calls to local social service agencies. Eventually she found me a bed in a battered women's shelter that would allow me to bring the children and stay for a maximum of seven days.

I was besotted with the milky clean, floral smells of my perfect new baby. I was too weary for tears. I knew only that I had to survive for the children's sake. It was months before I allowed myself to feel the depth of my own despair at having been abandoned with two very small children, myself twenty-three, and still a young woman.

November 2003

I AGONIZED. I snuck furtively down the toy aisle of the local supermarket with self-amused guilt, purposefully averting my eyes from the girls' section, and trying to find a suitable toy for a two-year-old on the other side of the aisle. Action toys. Armed soldiers and cars. I found nothing. Unbidden, I spied a pink baby-doll stroller on top of the pink plastic dolls and purses, and sheepishly I wrestled it down, took it to the cashier, and brought it home, hoping the whole time that no one I knew would see me.

You were delighted, of course. You played with the stroller and your baby dolls for two days without stopping. But the first thing you did was to put your favorite baby in the little pram, and roll her out to our courtyard garden to face the waterfall. And you stood there with her in knowing silence.

I was awed. I came to ask if you remembered when I had done the same for you and you looked at me incredulously, with that "Duh, Mom" look.

"Yes, Mommy, I 'member, I'm showing my baba the water."

December 10, 2003

IT IS THE TWO-YEAR ANNIVERSARY of the serendipitous
intersection of our lives.

They say the home of the soul is the eyes. Your eyes are
luminous, black marbles, pools of melted ebony; velvet
candles they shine out accusingly from a face that defines the
circle of a small moon. You pretend to sleep under a blanket
the size and weight of a storm cloud, but our adult voices in
your hospital cubicle cause you to turn your head and peer out
at us without expression. Like a moonbeam. Clear, piercing,
achingly strong light is coming from your hospital crib.

Why did I go to Johannesburg General Hospital, that
monolith of a building, sitting imperiously on top of the
Parktown ridge? Why did I expect that darkness would
surround you? Some residue of the foulness of the crime
committed against you? What icy pain gripped at my heart
from the moment of that first phone call on that so ordinary
December morning?

"I have permission to visit the baby in the hospital—do
you want to come?" I heard my friend's words before I fully
recognized her voice.

"Yes, of course."

What baby? That baby? What hospital? What is this permission thing?

"I'll meet you there? Where?"

I answered with a resoluteness that I scarcely felt, with a strength that was ebbing away on the sandy beach of my fears even before I rang off on the call.

My Special Girl

And by this chaste blood so unjustly stain'd.

SHAKESPEARE, "THE RAPE OF LUCRETIA"

LUCRETIA'S VIOLATION MOVED THE ROMANS to exile a King. Who can I send into exile to avenge you?

The morning light of this late autumn day is pallid and late, even the birds are lazy, the wind is singing at the sun before they awake.

Bump, pause, the patter patter of two-year-old feet on the carpet. I see you standing at the threshold of my bedroom door; I don't need to open my eyes. I pretend I'm still sleeping. But I see you pause, your wooly hair in disarray, your pink flowered pajamas wrinkled, that thumb in your mouth, your dirty white blanket trailing loyally behind you.

"Mommy. You sleeping? I want to get in Mommy's Bed. I want to sleep with Mommy."

You climb indecorously over my head, blanket and thumb. You snuggle into the covers, snuggle with unfettered delight into the smell of me, the musky scent of security, of mother comfort. With your cold little brown feet on my stomach you notice that I am not wearing pajamas. You strip—bottoms, top, urine-damp training pants go flying with determined effort onto the floor.

Now we are two naked little girls under the covers on a sleepy half-lit Saturday morning. You are too happy to be still. You wiggle like a puppy in your happiness. I wake up suddenly with a deep-throated growl, like a Mama Bear, growling and tickling you under your fat arms until you helplessly dissolve into squeals and screams of little girl laughter. Breathing heavily we wrap up in your blanket, which smells of urine and yeast, like day-old bread left out in the sun.

I talk softly into the top of your head. "You are my Special Girl. Do you know why you are my Special Girl?" I ask, and you nod and shake your head just slightly, and suck contentedly on your finger and burrow into my neck.

"I went to the hospital to see you. And when I saw you I said, 'Oh! Look at that Special Baby.' And I picked you up and hugged you and patted you on your little back. And I said to the doctor, 'Can I take this Special Baby home? Can I take her home and be her Mommy?' And the doctor said, 'Yes, you can take home that Special Baby and be her Mommy.'"

You lie still. Your breath is quiet and sweet, and musty like the pleasant smell of slightly decaying roses against my ear.

ENDNOTES

[1] Fifty-one percent of all profits from the sales of this book will be used for research, prevention, and treatment of child sexual abuse through The Princess Trust, www.princesstrust.com.

[2] Not her real name.

[3] With my apologies to Hans Christian Andersen, and thanks to Mom.

[4] Thanks to Yeshi Newman, sister midwife from Berkeley.

[5] Alcántara, Isabel, and Sandra Egnolff. *Frida Kahlo and Diego Rivera* (New York, London: Prestel Publishing, 2001).

[6] Thanks to Lara Foot Newton, writer-director of the play "Tshepang."

[7] The references in the following Selected Bibliography are in support of this paper, Ford, C. (2003). "Infant Rape and the Deconstruction of Predatory and Impulsive Masculinity." Presentation for Sex and Secrecy Conference, Johannesburg.

SELECTED BIBLIOGRAPHY

Bilblarz, Timothy J., and Adrian E. Raftery. (1999). "Family Structure, Educational Attainment, and Socioeconomic Success: Rethinking the 'Pathology of Matriarchy'" *American Journal of Sociology* Volume 105, Issue 2, 321–365.

Chisholm, James S. (1993). "Death, Hope, and Sex: Life-History Theory and the Development of Reproductive Strategies." *Current Anthropology* Volume 34, Issue 1, 1-24.

De Mause, Lloyd. (1993). "The History of Child Abuse." Speech given to the *British Psychoanalytic Society*, London.

Doss, Brian D. (1998). "The multicultural masculinity ideology scale: validation from three cultural perspectives." *Sex Roles: A Journal of Research*, May.

Haniff, Nesha Z. (1998). "Violence Against Men and Women in the Caribbean: The Case of Jamaica." *Journal of Comparative Family Studies* Volume 29, Issue 2, 361.

Posel, Deborah. (2003). "Getting the Nation Talking about Sex: Reflections on the Politics of Sexuality and 'Nation-Building' in Post-Apartheid South Africa." (Work-in-progress Research).

Sideris, Tina. (2003). "Non-violent men in violent communities: Negotiating the head and the neck." (Unpublished manuscript).

Snider, Laureen. (1998). "Toward safer societies: punishment, masculinities and violence against women." *British Journal of Criminology* Volume 38, Winter.

Wood, Gale Goldberg and Susan E. Roche. (2001). "Situations and Representations: Feminist Practice with Survivors of Violence." *Families in Society: The Journal of Contemporary Human Services* Volume 82, Issue 6, 583-591.

PHOTO CREDIT: DARRYL CHRISS

The author with her oldest son Juma.

CLAUDIA J. FORD HAS THIRTY YEARS' EXPERIENCE in international development management and training, and has worked in most of the countries of Latin America, the Caribbean, the Middle East, South Asia, South East Asia, East and Southern Africa. Her specialties include health, family planning, HIV / AIDS, democratic institution building, and women's empowerment.

Ford is currently conducting research on transformation and gender equity, household economics, gender, poverty, and community-based natural resource management. She is a senior lecturer at the University of the Witwatersrand. Ford is the founder and director of The Princess Trust, a South African charity that deals with the issue of infant rape and child sexual abuse. Ford lives with her family in Johannesburg, South Africa.